LIFE AFTER

Life After

Finding strength and spirit in unexpected change

ANNA MITCHELL HALL

Cane Mill Press

First Printing, 2021

Library of Congress Control Number: 2021922996

ISBN/SKU 978-1-7375604-2-5
EISBN 978-1-7375604-3-2

Cane Mill Press
Scottdale, GA 30079
www.canemillpress.com
editor@canemillpress.com

CONTENTS

With gratitude to Jim, my husband, partner, and best friend, and with thanks to all who have helped me walk through change over the years.

~ 1 ~

PREFACE

Everything old has passed away; see, everything has become new.
-2 Corinthians 5:17-19, New Revised Standard Version

Change seems to be waiting for us around every corner.

In 2020, the world came to a halt due to a global pandemic. School buildings shuttered, and learning moved online. Work went remote for many, and, for those working in essential roles, the threat of illness made every single day stranger and more stressful than the one before. Most of us stopped socializing with those outside our home, going months without seeing our beloved family and friends. Our favorite traditions, from dining out to sports to church, were interrupted and reinterpreted. We attended worship in our homes while simultaneously singing God's song in the strange lands of Zoom and YouTube. By our microphones and cameras, we sat down and wept with joy at weddings, baptisms, and ordinations, and with sorrow at funerals and the final services of dying congregations. This change was at a speed and on a scale that humanity had not seen in at least a few generations.

As I write this, my family and I have been vaccinated against the virus and received our boosters. While I am celebrating these steps that hopefully move us toward normality, I am still grieving all we have lost and unclear about what the future will hold. I am clear, however, that the future will contain further unexpected changes for me and for my faith community.

We humans have a mixed and complicated relationship with change. In the United States, we careen from electing leaders promising change to electing those dedicated to reversing those changes. We want the change we want, but only if those things that comfort us can remain the same.

Despite our individual personal and political attitudes, change is inevitable. No president, or anyone else, has enough power to prevent change. Every generation since the industrial revolution has lived lives that were greatly changed from their parents and grandparents. Technological change accelerated the process even faster in the twentieth century, to the point that each micro-generation is notable for what technology has been a part of their lives since birth. Yet, the skills needed for surviving and thriving during change are the same ones that allowed every one of our ancestors to live into their new generation.

What does this have to do with modern life?

Everything.

If you are alive, you will face frequent and often unexpected change. If you are Christian, like I am, change will be a part of your faith journey. Change is a fundamental element of Christianity, a faith claimed by generation upon generation that came before us. Some Christian voices might say Christianity only speaks against change and worships a God and set of rules that can never change. Yet more and more people are realizing God still speaks and speaks in new ways.

I am reminded of a poem by Jalaluddin Rumi, a Sufi poet who lived almost 1000 years ago. The poem, "The Guest House," in a beloved translation by Coleman Barks, refers to life as a guest house, where the arrival of any change can be welcomed as a beloved guest and potential guide. While we cannot control when and how change will come to visit, if we are willing to welcome such an unexpected visitor, we may hear in its voice a new awareness, guiding us in our next steps, and yes, even helping us learn to embrace change.

~ 2 ~

THE CHALLENGE OF CHANGE

Unexpected change occurs daily all around us. Highly publicized examples of life change make headlines, from celebrity divorces to political leaders facing scandal. These examples may seem dramatic, yet any time we encounter a big change, this encounter can be a profound experience. While our initial reactions may be negative, especially for those of us who prefer to know what to expect at every turn, these changes can be more than trials to get through. In this book, I explore how change is a part of our spiritual journeys, and this work is grounded in my own journey as a progressive Christian pastor and consultant. Along this journey, I have come to believe each unexpected change can be a chance to learn more about how to follow the God that makes all things new.

Like the disciples, who struggled to adapt after Jesus' death and resurrection, with the added challenge of struggling to understand much of the wisdom He had left with them, every day, we are charged as Christians with continuing in the face of losing a job, a relationship, or changes in where and how we live and work. This book is for you, so you can learn from the change you are facing now and from changes you will face in your future. This book is for anyone who wants to listen to and learn from God during all the changes life will throw at them.

Everyone deals with change differently, and some are more comfortable with change than others. Often the way change transforms us (or does not) depends on whether we see it as a good or bad thing.

Personally, I hate change. When I hear about something that is changing and out of my control—something at work, my bus route, a technology I use, or a tool I rely on—I get very weird. I start to feel all hot and flushed. I immediately get aggravated with whoever caused this change or the person delivering the news of the change. I begin thinking of who I can blame and where I can lodge an official complaint. I generally come to acceptance at some point, but my initial reaction is 100% fight or flight. Certainly, as a researcher of pastoral transitions and someone who really enjoys observing and participating in organizational change, I obviously do not hate all change. Yet when you get down to the nitty-gritty of changes that affect my life and are not in my control in any way whatsoever, I am not a fan.

In my years of studying and working on change, though, I found out a few things about change that shifted my perspective. I began to understand:

Change can and should be an integral part of any faith journey.

Change can be a living devotional.

Change can be the raw material that is transformed into new insights and awareness.

Change can bring us closer to our fellow Jesus followers, from the beginning of our faith until today.

Change can be a powerful tool for our personal and congregational development.

So, how can we shift our perspective on change? How can we move from seeing it as an unpleasant visitor to a welcome gift from God?

Change and our Christian Story

In my work, I am often immersed in the stories of Jesus and the other characters in the Bible. What I have discovered in those stories is that change is built into the story of Christianity.

The disciples experienced change on the road to Emmaus (Luke 24:13–32). They were working to process what they believed had happened to Jesus, having heard things beyond their comprehension and possibly beyond their belief. They could not incorporate this new information, the words of the women and their vision telling them Jesus was alive, their checking the tomb and finding it empty, into what they believed had happened, that Jesus had been killed by the authorities and would be with them no more on this journey they had chosen because of his call.

Even when they met who they believed to be a stranger on the road, they could not process that this stranger was, in fact, Jesus. Assuming him a true stranger, they told him the whole story. The story of the trauma of their beloved rabbi being put to death, the story of their hopes and dreams for him, the story of their ongoing confusion. Jesus had some more lessons for them. He told them that not believing the women, or their own eyes, was foolish and slow of heart. That not taking this new information and incorporating it with what they knew of the scriptures was the wrong path.

But despite all these disorienting experiences, it was not until Jesus broke bread with them, as he had so many times before, that they found a new understanding that while Jesus was killed, he had not left them. He was walking with them into their future.

How many times are we faced with change, with new information, only to compare it with what we already know and either discard new conflicting data or doubt the data's truthfulness or relevance? We are just like Jesus' disciples every single day. We second guess and resist change at every turn. We doubt the good news, or God news, in change, until we have a transforming experience or insight that opens our eyes.

The problem is that too often, we do not have those mountain-top experiences. We go along unchanged, or resisting change, and never learning how God may be speaking to us in the process.

Big Changes Ahead

Like the disciples, who struggled with change after Jesus' death and resurrection, with the added challenge of struggling to understand much of the wisdom He had left with them, we each face transitions throughout our lives. During such transitions, some people find their faith tried or strengthened by their experiences during the transition.

But even when their experiences have the potential for profound learning, people consistently interpret their experiences considering their preexisting beliefs. Struggling with any information that conflicted with those beliefs, seeking out research and information to shore up their preexisting beliefs, they put all new information in a box marked "Don't need, don't want," high up on a shelf somewhere.

We often want to see a situation in the best light, so we ignore information that might be more negative. We want to think of ourselves one way, so we cannot figure out how to claim a new identity. Even those of us who believe we are forward-thinking can struggle to leave behind the old and make room for the new.

Changing our Minds

The disciples could not take in the new information of the women's testimony, the empty tomb, the appearance of Jesus. Not at first. They had new information, sure, but they took it, compared it to what they believed to be true, and dismissed any parts that did not fit.

We all do this.

Brain research has suggested that people experience genuine pleasure--the same brain chemical released from pleasure or a substance high--when processing information that supports their be-liefs (Wong, 2017).

Before the 2004 elections in the United States, researchers asked 30 men with strong political feelings to evaluate seemingly self-contradictory statements made by both George W. Bush and John Kerry. The Republicans were critical of Kerry, the Democratic subjects were critical of Bush, yet both neatly avoided criticizing "their guy." Emory researchers found, using MRI scans, that the part of the brain most associated with reasoning was inactive during this process. Yet the parts responsible for emotions, conflict resolution, and making judgments about morality were very active. Once the men arrived at a conclusion that fit their pre-existing preference for a candidate, their reward and pleasure centers lit right up (Westen et al., 2006).

Such brain imaging research demonstrates that strongly-held beliefs are not only difficult to change, but that brain processes actively resist changing them. Parts of the brain that handle reasoning are less active when we are faced with information that challenges our strongly-held positions. We experience an emotional shock, almost as if we are a rat in a science experiment choosing the wrong path in the maze. The most active areas as we take in this challenging information are those dedicated to handling emotions and resolving conflict, followed by activity in the pleasure area when the conflict is believed to be resolved. We love this feeling of rejecting the new information or making it match what we believe.

In some ways, we are just rats in a maze of life, avoiding the shock of information that conflicts with our beliefs to get to the pleasure of reaffirming what we believe to be true. This is the challenge we have with our experiences of change. We go in with one idea of what is or should be unfolding and have an exceedingly difficult time opening ourselves to any new information from the change that, while it may be shocking or unexpected, can be one of our greatest sources of learning.

Yet we are called by the stories of our faith to transcend our instincts to take the safer path and avoid the shock. In fact, our faith is permeated with the idea of *metanoia*, which can be defined as a spiritual change of heart. Although often translated as repentance in Biblical texts, metanoia is an idea that more closely parallels what we would now call transformational learning, a change in thinking which changes the way we live.

Learning from Experience

For many people, learning from change, if it happens at all, is not transformative. Our frames of belief and understanding persist in the face of informal and incidental learning, despite experiences and new knowledge that challenge those frames. People going through change interpret everything through the lens of their frame of reference, if the change even intersects with their frame at all.

Research suggests most learning is transactional rather than transformative (Mezirow, 2000). Transactional learning is where learning through experience only results in new skills or information. You may know someone who went through a change and obtained information or skills needed to move forward, but stopped before creating any new insights or understanding. Our disorienting experiences are likely to be interpreted through the lens of our frame of reference and reinforce it, rather than change it significantly.

We favor new information that agrees with us and discard anything that doesn't. Sometimes we enjoy confirmation so much we seek it out. More on that later.

Finding the Transformation

According to scholar Barbara J. Fleischer (2006), the entire biblical narrative of Jesus' encounters with the disciples describes a teacher preparing his students for a profoundly changed way of life. He challenged his listeners to see a new reality of graciousness, transform their perspectives, and live according to this broader vision of life. Fleischer compares this way of changing the disciples' minds to the theory of transformative learning, which says that learning which transforms our beliefs and actions must be disorienting.

There is no way to get to the transformation without the disorientation.

And Jesus' life and words continually provoked disorientation in his followers, challenging their small views of God and how others were lacking in the eyes of God. The beautiful thing about the transformative lessons of Jesus is that they not only changed the disciples but confronted the small-minded and oppressive power structures of the time. These teachings led to Jesus' death at the hands of those authorities. Then we find ourselves back again on the road to Emmaus, as disciples who are finally disoriented enough to see through their shock toward the lessons of following Jesus on a post-resurrection journey. They were able to change their minds. And so can we.

In the following chapters, you will hear my stories and the stories of others who have navigated unexpected change. How we all learned or did not learn from our experiences. And whether we found ourselves transformed. These stories will serve as our companions throughout the book, as we explore how to not only navigate unexpected changes successfully but how to use them as an opportunity for transformation, as a chance to follow Jesus down a new road.

Let's get traveling.

Reflection Questions:

How do you feel when things in your life change?

Are you thrown for a loop? Or do you love the feeling of navigating new territory?

~ 3 ~

THE POWER OF CHANGE

Learning from experience is an essential part of the Christian faith journey. We all have stories of experiences that awakened us to a new way of thinking. Some of those experiences are big, like spending a night wrestling with fear in hopes of grabbing a blessing for the days to come, or an appointment spent receiving a good or bad diagnosis. Others are small, like a new coworker, a change in neighborhood, or just growing older. Our reactions to these experiences can vary. We don't learn in healthy ways every time we experience change.

As Christians, we are called to new lives every day, and the rhythm of our years are shaped by a story of death and new life. So, grabbing hold of the transformation possible in the changes that come into our lives can be a crucial part of our faith formation. Jesus calls us to be willing to be disoriented, and to then re-evaluate our current beliefs. To repent and change our minds. And learning, at its heart, literally changes our minds.

Yet all too often, we get stuck.

We never reevaluate the things we think we know. We fail to take in new information in a way that allows us to change our minds. Sometimes we simply stop, stuck in our tracks, refusing to change when change comes, railing at the winds.

Other times, we may learn and even be transformed by the smallest changes.

A friend of mine, David, who works as a business consultant, had his eyes opened to a community of homeless men living in a park after he merely changed the way he drove to work. He formed relationships with them and eventually, in partnership with the congregation where he was a member, founded and directed an organization called The River, dedicated to helping people without homes through relationship-building with those who are housed. This organization works with other local groups to help neighbors who live outside access both services and a community of caring friends to improve their quality of life. In some cases, this means they move off the street into housing. In other cases, they remain outside for now but benefit from their new community in terms of jobs or benefits needed to live as well as possible for their situation. More recently, David helped found a community center in a neighborhood where people are at a high risk of displacement and homelessness, to work on the systemic issues underlying precarious housing situations. A simple alteration of his route to work has now impacted many of David's friends, both those who live outside and those who share his vision for relationships across boundaries. We never really know when change will bring an opportunity for amazing things.

Barriers to Learning

It is obvious we do not always learn, even in very disorienting situations.

Our human brains have some natural resistance to change. Recent neuroscience research can explain some of this. Our brains try extremely hard to protect us from danger. One way our brains do this is to flag anything that conflicts with our existing understandings as an error. This is done by activating our emotional brain activity in the amygdala and decreasing our rational brain activity in the prefrontal cortex. New information is harder to process and can exhaust our memory and processing. Our brains also pay more attention to negative input than positive. This is important in learning to avoid touching hot stoves, but counterproductive in other areas of our lives, particularly in our need to press through discomfort of change to learn what it has to teach us (Scarlett, 2016).

In an example of these brain processes at work, a man that I interviewed as part of my dissertation was very troubled by the changing attitudes toward same sex marriage in his church and denomination. He sought out a great deal of information on the changing policies regarding same sex marriage within his church's larger denomination. Yet no matter how much time he spent investigating, he reported that he could not find any information on the arguments for legalizing same sex marriage within the church structure. The information on these other positions was out there, a cursory internet search on my part found them quickly, but his frame of reference regarding what was acceptable Christian practice did not allow him to acknowledge them at all. His approach to gathering information, in fact, served to reinforce his existing frame of reference that there could be no logical justification for the opposing position.

To be clear, evaluating evidence and not changing one's mind on a big issue is completely okay. Being blind to discovering the arguments of the opposing position is the issue, as it prevents one from a greater understanding of the world in which we live. Without some intervention, changes will not always lead to learning that is healthy and beneficial.

I have included in the following chapters a number of strategies, practices and considerations which can help you learn in ways that support your faith during or after challenging changes. These include:

- celebration and ritual
- reflection
- discernment and direction

- acceptance
- mindfulness
- sabbath
- grief
- shame
- community, and
- family.

These will become the supplies you pack for your journey into change. The contents of your suitcase, so to speak.

In the coming chapters, I explain why each of these are important and provide ideas about how to incorporate them into your life. You may need all of these or only a few to navigate the next big change in your life. You can read about them in order or feel free to jump around. I invite you to try each one on and see which are most natural for you, which are growing areas, and which may not be useful for you at this time.

However you explore them, I pray at least a few will be helpful for you in your journey through change.

Reflection Questions

Are some changes easier for you where others are frustrating, exhausting, or anxiety-producing? Which are the most challenging?

What differentiates "good change" from "bad change" for you?

~ 4 ~

INTERLUDE: RHYTHMS OF CHANGE

The first three approaches, celebration/ritual, reflection, and discernment/direction, form the core rhythm of navigating any change. To be successful in moving through and learning from change, we must first acknowledge the change through rejoicing or lamenting, using celebration and ritual to help us with this work. We must next go inward, discovering our own relationship to the change and to change in general, surfacing our beliefs and transforming them if needed, and playing in the realm of story to name those relationships and beliefs and connect them to ancient and modern stories that can be our guides. Finally, we must listen for the voice of spirit within to help us see what is next for us and begin traveling in our new direction. If you do nothing else when facing a big change, incorporating this rhythm into your life, even briefly, can help you learn and grow.

~ 5 ~

CELEBRATION AND RITUAL

At some point in our lives, we have all been anxiously awaiting the new year, a new start, a new chance at better things ahead. From ancient days, the turn of years or seasons has caused people to contemplate change, starting over, and how to live in the coming year. This can take the form of anything from monsters to prayer, to good luck rituals, to myriad ways of saying goodbye to the old and hello to the new.

The Monsters of Change
It was actually ancient solstice festivals that got us to the European monsters of the darkest time of year. The end of harvest and celebrations of seasons change included merrymakers going around in disguise, as long ago as holidays like Saturnalia in ancient Rome, when people used disguises to hide signs of their class or rank, to reverse social orders and mix freely with one another. In Tudor England, the lord of misrule was crowned during the days after Christmas when servants were at their leisure. He led days of mischief and partying for these hard workers who had few other times free for celebration. These celebrations got so rowdy as they came to this continent through the European colonists that early Boston residents dressed as animals, painted their faces, drank wildly, and acted out in the streets. They danced at doorways as

carolers and begged for food, alcohol and money as wassailers. These parties got so wild that the Puritans banned Christmas from 1659--1681!

But about those monsters: Traditions in Appalachia and Pennsylvania held that such masked and costumed celebrants were fiends, called "belsnickels," and taught children that obedient behavior would keep them from becoming their prey. And because of popular culture, I'm sure you've heard of the Eastern European Krampus, who rather than leaving coal in stockings, kidnaps and eats bad children, or at minimum, takes them off to hell.

Interesting stories, to be sure, but what does all this have to do with navigating change? Why do we have such monstrous traditions accompanying the change in seasons, as things get so dark and then begin to return to life?

I don't know if you've heard of thin places, but these are geographies that are said to collapse the distance between heaven and earth, or between the material and the magical. I think perhaps the changing of the year is a temporal thin place, where we allow ourselves to live liminally, or in-between, playing with ideas of what's real and what's magical, what was and what is possible. And even what has been monstrous, so we can leave it far behind.

Language Older than Words

While I'm sure every one of you reading this has some family or personal traditions around at least one holiday or season (pumpkin-spice latte, anyone?), we often forget to honor the need for rituals and celebration to say our goodbyes and hellos when we are going through a change in our life.

So why has it been so important for human beings, from ancient times until today, to mark the changing year in these ways?

Research from brain science suggests reflection and ritual can be the first step in building the future we want to see. Andrew Newbert and Robert Waldman, in *How God Changes your Brain* (2009), observe that while popular media in recent years is full of conversation about affirmations and intentions having an almost magical quality, there are practical implications every time we imagine and ritualize ideas of our hoped-for future. They say the brain uses creative imagination in the frontal lobe to begin setting goals, which moves our brains, and us, closer to the future we dream of. Although imagination can seem fantastical, it serves a very important role in our mindset and the actions we take to reach our goals. To get there, we have to move beyond rumination on the potential pitfalls which can consume all our time, and focus on the possibility of success in order to keep moving forward. Neurologically, negative thinking activates our limbic system, which can then reinforce our anxiety and fear. We can strengthen the neural circuits for fear and anxiety, which I don't think is an exercise routine any of us are looking for. Conversely, if you stay focused on your goal through brain practices such as affirmation and meditation, you can actually alter the neural circuitry in your brain to make the possibility of success feel more real.

Rituals have been shown to be helpful in alleviating grief, reducing anxiety, and increasing confidence. This is still true when people claim that they do not believe rituals work. In experiments, researchers found rituals gave people a greater sense of acceptance, and that such a sense of control reduced feelings of grief (Norton and Gino, 2013). Most of the rituals they studied were personal, not religious or community based, involving things like writing on a paper and tearing it up or destroying old photographs. Any ritual, it appears, will do, even an arbitrary one designed by the researchers, to help increase a sense of acceptance and control after an unexpected loss. Rituals can look like communion at church, or burning old papers from the life we are leaving behind, or scattering stones in a stream. No matter the ritual, God is there with us as we remember, grieve, celebrate, or bless.

We can also find growth in changes when we allow time and space for ritual as we turn from our old road onto the new. This ritual may look like saying goodbye to a place or community that served us well but cannot be with us on our new road. It may look like acknowledging those parts of ourselves that we must leave behind. It may also look like celebrating and blessing the experiences that will come on this new road, recognizing God is in it all.

In *The Wild Edge of Sorrow: Rituals of Renewal and the Sacred Work of Grief* (2015), Francis Weller suggests that rituals are older than words and speak to us on nonverbal levels. Weller cites the work of author and ritual facilitator Z. Budapest in connecting us to our ancestors and nature through rituals. Weller also asserts that ritual repairs our souls, helping us remember and reestablish our inner rhythms and to place them once again in accord with the deeper cadence of our soul. In other words, rituals can help us find transformation even in difficult times. Rituals can help us move from feeling stuck into new directions.

We can use ritual to celebrate the past and bless a new opportunity to do God's work in a new way. Ritual can help us feel the sadness of the ending if we write their favorite memories on a stone and cast it into the water. Ritual can help us embrace our hopes for the future by allowing us to speak these hopes into the sacred. The only resources needed are a little creativity and openness to experimentation.

Those seasonal traditions I mentioned above, from revelry to monsters, to prayer, to new resolutions, bring us hope for the days to come, and ways to say goodbye to the struggles behind. They train our brain to focus on that which we hope for. And if we continue reflecting on that goal, that dream, that vision, that hope, we make it more likely in our brain, and thus, our lives, that it will come true. It turns out that hope is good for the soul. I recently read an article that pointed out that in Spanish, the word for "wait" is *espera* and the word for "hope" is *esperanza*. That feels obvious, but I'd never thought of it that way before.

What are some ways we can build in celebrations and rituals of grief and hope when facing a change?

Take the Time to Say Goodbye

We are called in times of change to leave our old routines behind and go into new territory, go, perhaps, where we don't belong. And in my view, this is worth one of those long goodbyes, the kind where you keep saying you're leaving and first stand up and talk some more, then you move toward the door and keep talking, then you're hanging out the door and still saying a few things, and the hosts follow you out to the driveway to wave and tell you to drive safe as you finally pull away. The kind where my uncle said as a child to my very talkative extended family members: "If you're going, go on."

Some ideas for goodbye rituals from seasonal celebrations around the world: In Denmark, they throw dishes at the doors of those they love to banish bad spirits. In Panama, some burn effigies of famous people to leave the old year and its spirits behind. In Scotland, they wave burning poles to represent the sun, purifying the coming year. In many Unitarian Universalist churches, a fire communion is offered around the new year to say goodbye to things we wish to leave behind by throwing them into the fire, while setting intentions for those things we want to see in the coming year.

We can't forget that goodbye often involves grief as well. I will explore this area more in a later chapter, but rituals can incorporate grief. Most years, I make time to attend a worship service designed for honoring grief during the winter holidays. Often called a Blue Christmas or Longest Night service, these are opportunities to acknowledge the reality of feeling sad, lost, or alone during these days when everyone else appears to be making merry. We hear readings to remind us both of the weeping mothers of Ramah and the ever presence of God. We celebrate our fragility by receiving gifts of treasured ornaments donated by those who wanted to pass along these breakable things that had somehow come through the years intact. I always come away feeling more whole, somehow, after the opportunity to say a sad farewell to those things I am grieving. This ritual reminds me that sadness, grief, and all the complicated emotions I carry are necessary for times of change.

Acknowledge and Celebrate the Past

No matter how young or old you are, you have a history that is worth celebrating.

What are the major turning points of your life, moments along the way where you made important decisions, faced challenges, and journeyed through change? Make a list of those moments and think about how you might speak those stories into this present season of change. Could you write them, draw them, make a collage?

Celebrate your triumphs and your challenges, as it takes both to make you who you are. All journeys, and the milestones along the way, are worth celebrating. Pay particular attention to recent challenges. Rather than pretending everything was hunky-dory until this current change, surface and honor the sticky situations that may be still echoing through the life of you. Without attention to your past, any new changes will not be fully processed in healthy ways. When we have unspoken truths, or "elephants in the room," our whole selves are not incorporated into the process of change, limiting transformation.

Who have been your "saints?" This may not be the language you use, but you may have people who have been stalwart supporters and friends along your life's journey. Whether you do this routinely or not, times of change are the perfect occasion for celebrating these folks. Take time to thank them or remember them, if they are no longer in your life.

Celebrate the pre-change life you are leaving behind. In churches I work with, we invite members to gather in small groups and write a eulogy for those things they may need to leave behind. What eulogy could you write for what you are leaving behind? What were gifts to you? What were challenges? How could you do them all justice by testifying to the role they played in your life. If you are feeling brave, read it to friends and family when you're done writing.

A few more ideas for your celebrations of the past: In my own family, growing up my mom and I always took time on New Year's Eve not to make resolutions but to reflect on our favorite memories from the past year, and make little books out of card stock to record those memories for the future. Or, celebrate as you would a birthday, in leaving the old year behind and greeting the new. Whether you are facing a retirement, the ending of a relationship or the leaving of a home, have some cake and tell stories with friends to honor all that you have gained from the past. Sing a few songs and/or tell stories together of your history. You will remember the celebrations long after the hard struggles have faded from memory, and those celebrations will become a part of your story going forward.

Get Rowdy and Ready to Say Hello

Finally, celebrate the new when appropriate! With every ending comes a new beginning, and often those events are worth celebrating. Once you discern what is next for you, honor that by naming it publicly along with your hopes and dreams for what lies ahead.

Throw another party! "Christen" the new thing with a bottle of champagne (or some non-alcoholic punch), cut a big red ribbon across some doors, or hold an open house party. Invite guests to write on index cards what they are most excited about and read them aloud in lieu of toasts.

Some further ideas from around the world: What are our Easter or Christmas celebrations in our churches and families other than an opportunity to rejoice in all the potential present in new life? Try using candles or eggs to represent new light and life. Or focus on the sweet possibilities ahead. One Jewish tradition includes apples and honey on Rosh Hashanah to symbolize God's blessing of a sweet year to come. What rituals can you think of to say hello to whatever is around the corner?

No matter what rituals we choose for our seasons of change, we're part of an ancient and powerful longing for a new way ahead of us.

I wish you good goodbyes, joyful celebrations, and rowdy hellos along your way.

Reflection Questions

When is the last time you threw a party to celebrate something new? What was the occasion? How did you celebrate?

Have you ever done a ritual to say goodbye to something in your life or mark a big change? What did you do? How did it feel?

~ 6 ~

REFLECTION

During times of change, it is important to remember the old saying, "Know thyself." We often struggle with change when we do not face the change standing strongly in our own story and identity.

Increasing Understanding

To build our change skills, we first understand how we respond to change. We do not hear much about the internal journeys of the folks in the Bible, but we certainly know how it feels when such an unexpected change happens to us. We almost always respond negatively at first. Our own brains are responsible for much of our negative reactions to unexpected change. Science has found that as we go throughout our daily routines, our brains anticipate the next most likely event. Most of the time, this serves us well, saving us time and energy in navigating our lives and world (Neal, et al., 2011).

When that next most likely event does not occur, our brain begins secreting strong chemicals that make us extra alert and ready to act. These chemicals make us feel on edge and uncomfortable, training us to dislike unexpected change. To get through this feeling, we start to sort through this unexpected event and try to categorize it. In truly unexpected life changes this can be difficult, and our brains begin to exist in a state of uncertainty, which we experience as fear or anxiety. We start to assign labels of threat or blame (Rock, 2008). We feel out of control. As humans, we thrive when we have a sense of control. Some things in our lives will never be self-chosen. Illness, job loss, death of a loved one. And research also suggests that the more we feel that life events are out of our control, the less positive action we are likely to take.

Mice, in a seemingly random situation where there is no way to predict whether they will receive a shock or some cheese, eventually become listless and just lay there without taking any action at all (Landgraf, 2015). People who experience a negative career shock, such as downsizing or transfer to an unwanted location, were less likely to take positive action on improving skills through graduate training (Seibert, et al., 2013). Sadly, the more we are shocked by negative life events, the less likely we can be to shape our lives through positive choices. The challenge is getting past feeling out-of-control and fearful so that we can move toward re-orientation into a new understanding.

Thankfully, this sort of disorientation is a key factor in our transformation. Transformational learning only occurs in the context of disorientation. One of our key tasks in congregations is helping members understand that these feelings are part of the process. Like grief, the only way to get through it is to go through it. When we avoid these feelings, cover them up with dysfunctional behaviors or try to skip past them, we fail to learn and be transformed. But if we are trained to expect these feelings and how to respond, we may be able to sit with the discomfort long enough to learn.

Confession

To grow during times of change, we must acknowledge, I might even say confess, our discomfort with change. We are all planners. We may not be especially skilled at planning, but we all do it. We envision what is ahead for us, and we start thinking about how we will navigate that future. We have dreams and hopes for that future, and we paint vivid pictures of that future in our minds. But of course, things do not always go as planned.

And one of the hardest types of change for us to handle is when life makes us take such a radical detour that it completely upends all those plans. When life interrupts what we had thought our future would be -- we get laid off from a job that we loved, or we find that we hate the job we always wanted, or a significant relationship ends through death or a breakup, or we realize that a significant life partnership is not likely for us. We have an unexpected pregnancy, or we find that we cannot have children. We have a health crisis that limits our activities or devastates our savings, or a family member's health forces us into full time care giving. Our church goes through an organizational crisis or loses a long-serving pastor. There are so many ways our life and future can refuse to turn out as we had planned.

Molly Baskette, in her book *Standing Naked before God* (2015), addresses our need to tell our stories to people who are present to the possibility of really knowing us. Her church practiced confessing to each other regularly in worship, preparing and telling stories of their sins and vulnerabilities and what came next. Doing so trained the congregation in understanding and practicing that no aspect of ourselves should be left out of our practice of faith. Baskette cites Henri Nouwen's call for us to "put our wounds into the service of others." We may not know who might be healed in the hearing of it, if we share our stories of crisis and change, and how we responded, good or bad. We can know that the collective will be transformed by this radical act of presence and witness, every time.

When was the last time you confessed your attitude toward and relationship with change to a friend or family member? Why not try it this week?

Examine Your Beliefs

When we are faced with tragedy, with earthquakes of loss, with events so painful and troubling that we are shaken to our cores, we often get confused about just where God is in our lives. What we believe can make all the difference in steering through such challenging seasons. When life hits us hard, we may feel we have lost God's favor somehow, that the unfairness of it all proves that the bargain we thought we were making by keeping God's commandments was written with disappearing ink. Or that God is punishing us somehow, for all those times we failed to be perfect and did the wrong thing. We may feel guilt that we are so affected by our circumstances, and ashamed that God is not speaking because we are not able to keep the faith unwaveringly during a dark time.

So, which are we to believe about God? When earthquakes of life and loss rock us to our very core: is God the cause of the earthquakes, or is God the loving mother who is holding a cup of refreshment for our dry mouths as we struggle to catch our breath, reeling from tragedy? Is God the cause of the tragedy or is God the mother hen who gathers us under her wings to hold us until we feel safe again? Is God the one who takes from us, or is God the one who offers a healing holding embrace as we process what we have lost?

In good times, we often attribute our fortune, our blessings to God, despite knowing that there are many who are just as faithful as we who have very little money, or success, or romantic love. And these are only a few of our lived theologies. Not all these theologies are ones we can truly live with. Not live the lives God has envisioned for us, anyway. Some of these theologies keep us imprisoned in guilt or self-hatred or fear and judgment of others. We can't live as free and beloved children of God.

About a decade ago, after many years of infertility, I had a very complicated pregnancy and our daughter died at two weeks old. That was the hardest time of my life. Then, a few years back, we had another hard year in my little family, with a series of medical tests, surgeries, procedures, and car repairs. It seemed like almost every member of our family, our dogs and car included, was falling apart in some way. Then, after a fairly easy 2019, these last two years of pandemic have been challenging, to say the least. We are all okay now, but I spent much of the last decade feeling exhausted and fragile. I absolutely struggled at times to figure out what I believed during my hardest days. However, through it all, I found comfort in these things: God was with us. God loved us. God wept with us. God was also moving in me, calling me toward the way forward, if I was willing to listen.

One scripture that I often think about during seasons like that is John 1.

In the beginning was the Word.

The book of the Bible we call John was probably written over a long period, years after Jesus' life and ministry, by an author or a group of authors whose name may or may not have been John. The book emerged from a whole different tradition and community than the other three gospels that tell the life of Jesus, Matthew, Mark, and Luke. It concerns itself with the identity of Jesus and how much Jesus claimed about that identity while alive. It was possibly written to serve as a public proclamation of Jesus' role as Messiah.

This Greek term we translate as "the word," Logos, interjected right here at the beginning, about the beginning, captures the cross cultural and cross mythical nature of this tale. If written to tell a wide audience about Jesus in the 2nd century in the middle east, it has elements designed to make all of them uncomfortable. Beth Scibienski reflects on how this passage troubles the way the Greeks and the Jews of the time would have conceived of creation, by offering a new creation story with elements of both. The Greeks believed creation involved Chaos first, then Night, then love, then light. Big abstract ideas, writ large and bringing the world into being. The Jews of this time believed creation involved one God persona, creating light in a formless void, then the material world, then creatures, and calling it all good. Concrete, personal, material, dirt and earth and skin.

But John says, no. Word first.

Creative force of the universe first, then present, always, always, always with God and in all creation and through all creation, and especially through the human baby born in Jesus. This would have been way too personal for the Greeks and way too abstract for the Jews. It would have shocked them, troubled them, and probably delivered on the author's intention—to get their attention.

And how does it ring true for us? For now? For our real beliefs about life and creation? Does it get our attention? Do we believe the word, the life, the light are in us? And have always been in us? Or is that just as foreign to us as to the 2nd century audiences of Greeks and Jews?

In studying a Bible passage, I often like to read it in several translations. This comes partly from my affection for hearing classic texts and stories presented in many ways, from modern urban settings of Shakespeare to hip hop recitations of American history. But I also think this is a great way to help our ears break through and hear new things out of often familiar passages. For today's text, I was curious how one of my favorite Gospel interpreters, Clarence Jordan, would change things up a bit in his *Cotton Patch Gospels* (1970). *The Cotton Patch Gospels*, interpretations of the Jesus story set in the American south, were written by Jordan, a farmer, agricultural scientist, Greek scholar, and counterculture creator. He founded an interracial Christian farming community in deep south Georgia, near where I'm from, back in 1942. That community was firebombed and boycotted for daring to interpret Christianity as calling for cooperation and integration between the races. His gospel interpretations were written to trouble that water, to get their attention, those of the firebombs and boycotts and even polite conversations about all this trouble being made at Koinonia. I like his interpretations of the Gospels because he has a way of making them sound like a story someone might tell around one of my family's holiday tables. Here's how he tells it:

> *When time began, the Idea already was. The Idea was at home with God, and the Idea and God were one. This same Idea was at home with God when time began. Through him the universe was made,*

and apart from him not one thing came to be. In him was life, and the life was humanity's light. And the light shines on in the darkness, and the darkness never quenched it. (Jordan, 1970, p. 74)

This light, present from the beginning, is made of humanity's life, and enlightens every man. And the best news of all, this light shines on in the darkness, and the darkness never quenches it. The darkness of racism and firebombing and boycotts and the evil of ordinary people can not quench the light.

Can this be our comfort when we are grieving, or scared of a change, or when we simultaneously wish for a fresh start and fear those fresh starts will quickly get mired in so much life stuff, or when we feel like change means we're moving in reverse? Can we hold to this indwelling light and life when failure and darkness seem all around?

Sacred Stories

To incorporate good theology about change into your beliefs, it can be helpful to weave stories of change into your spiritual journey. There are numerous stories in the Bible and in Christian history about journeys through unexpected change. I've told you a couple of my favorites above. Do you have stories that ground your faith in times of change?

Abraham is commanded by God, "Go from your country and your kindred and your father's house to the land that I will show you." (Genesis 12:1) He thought he would live out the rest of his days in Ur. He was elderly. But Abraham went anyway.

Moses hears from God, "I am the Lord; tell Pharaoh king of Egypt all that I am speaking to you." (Exodus 6:29) Moses responded by calling himself a "nobody" and doubted he could do such a thing. God told him again and again that he was the one to speak. So Moses went anyway.

Ruth followed her mother-in-law to a new land to ensure she was cared for. Naomi told her not to come. Ruth would be a for-

eigner in this new land, a stranger to all but Naomi. Ruth went anyway (Ruth 1)

We hear in Genesis about Jacob and Esau—about a time when
a man, Jacob, feared his brother Esau so much that he was willing
to sacrifice half his flocks and family as human shields, sending
them out before him just in case his brother was feeling vengeful
and murderous. Jacob, though, had an encounter on the road as
he waited his turn to meet his brother, an encounter that changed
him. He wrestled with a being that he called an angel all night.
This experience marked his body and changed his name. How do
we know of this transformation? He named the place it happened
Penuel, which means "I have seen God face to face, and my life is
preserved." (Genesis 32:30) In this way, his story was told through
future generations whenever anyone asked the origin of the name.

Jesus' movement was grounded in story. Jesus came and told a
new story about God's relationship with humanity, a different story
than the governmental or religious authorities of his time. Brian
McLaren (2017) says that for organizing religion, words are important, but even more important are stories. McLaren also observes
that in the foundational stories of Christian faith, humans, and Jesus, are constantly on the move, in transition. The stories Jesus and
his followers told along the way, their public theology, cast a com-
pelling vision for where they were headed.

We hear in Luke about a leper, healed by Jesus, as were so many.
But this encounter changes more than his health. He is filled with
gratitude, and we know this because he walks back to tell his story
and give thanks to the man who changed his life (Luke 17:11-19)

In my own research, a woman named Gail told of lessons learned
from a time when people shared stories at her church.

*"I think I learned how important it is for us to share our personal stories
as far as like our spiritual journey.... That kind of let me see that everyone is
so different even though it may not be diverse in age or race, culture, back-
ground or whatever, it's very different and where everyone comes from, like
their perspective, but at the same time it's relatable."*

Simply talking about change experiences in a group can help surface the emotions and impressions that change brings.

Stories have a way of cultivating our moral imagination, or our capacity to bring creative futures to life (Lederach, 2005). While the world tells stories of domination and fear, we can tell stories of creativity and hope from the Bible or from our lives. Tell your stories— to yourself and others. The only way to bring new people into a story is to tell it to them. In fact, our friends may need reminders of these stories too! You can share new stories of walking through change on social media and in conversation with neighbors. Perhaps you will record stories of hope and distribute them through a podcast or other medium. You may write letters to the editor or submit a column to your local paper.

If you tell the stories of how change is an essential part of spiritual journey, you will not only internalize this embrace of change but help others in your orbit grapple with changes they face in their lives as individuals and in organizations. Talk about good news!

Reflection Questions:

What can you do to examine your relationship to change? Your beliefs that are affecting your experience of change?

How do you tell stories in your family or friend group? What stories do you tell? Could you incorporate confessing your challenges with change and sharing the stories that inspire you?

~ 7 ~

DISCERNMENT AND NEW
DIRECTION

During times of change, we are called to leave old roads behind. Even family, even friends, even community, we are called to leave things behind and follow Jesus down new roads ahead. In fact, the story of Jesus is the story of a community who thought things would go one way, toward a future as a community following a beloved rabbi around, hearing his teachings and loving their neighbors under his guidance—only to find their leader killed by political forces and forced to make a new way without him.

How do we make a new way in times of great change? How do we listen, discern, see the signs of the right next step?

A Still, Small Voice

Elijah, the prophet, spends his life telling the King through signs and prophecies that God thinks the northern kingdom of Israel is seriously on the wrong track . Although this work is highly unpopular, as you can imagine, and often leads to danger for Elijah, he feels sustained in this calling by God's continued presence in his life and God's equipping him to work signs and miracles. Yet in our story, he has been threatened with death by the king's wife, and this reversal of circumstances forces him to flee from his old life in terror. He heads out into the desert, in fear for his life. He is suffering so, from the conditions out in the desert and from feeling himself and his work abandoned by God, that he prays that he would die. He is crying out that he has tried to do everything God wanted, and still, terrible things have happened, and he feels he just can't go on. I wonder how many of us have ever felt so confused and hopeless.

But with Elijah, that's not the end of the story. God provides food for him and an angel commands him to eat it, so he will go on living. Elijah's prayers for death are not granted. At this point, God does something very interesting. Elijah is told to go out and listen for God. A great wind, and an earthquake, and a fire appear to Elijah, but in all those, he does not hear God. How must that have felt? He felt abandoned by God, and yet, when God tells him to go and listen for God's voice, he hears much noise, but no word from God. Talk about adding insult to injury.

But then, finally, he hears God.

When does he hear God? In the sheer silence. A still small voice asks him why he is in the wilderness praying for death. Elijah tells God exactly how he feels after all that has happened. And God tells him to go back. God tells him that there is work still to do. God tells him that he is called to return to others in community, not stay alone in the desert. (1 Kings 19)

So what can we learn from Elijah's story? What does it tell us about listening for God in the darkest of times -- and about how we can find our way out of the desert after the hurricanes, earthquakes and fires that life throws at us -- to reconnect with God and God's call for our lives?

Bringing Our Fears into the Conversation

It is tempting of course, after going through one of these life quakes, to want to stay still forever. It is safe where we are, or at least we make that deal with ourselves. Moving means risking, and we don't know if we can take any more loss or pain. But staying means staying buried, in the rubble of the past, in the rubble of our grief and fear.

We are instead called to bring our fears to God, and listen for God's call on our lives. Being Christians means being called to follow Jesus, being called to find what God is dreaming for our lives, and that doesn't end when we experience profound loss. God will love us if we stay hidden under God's wings for as long as we need to, but God also has big visions and dreams for us, that can't be lived into if we stay in hiding. Sometimes it can feel like we can't hear God's voice because we are hurting so much. And perhaps it isn't the voice we are used to hearing from God. But I think about real earthquakes, when rescuers are searching for survivors. They know they may not hear that person's usual hearty hello. Sometimes only a faint whisper or tapping.

And yet they continue seeking.

And sometimes they find.

We sometimes hear stories about rescuers finding survivors long after the disaster, under the rubble. If they had ceased to seek and listen after a few days, when most people would have believed all hope was lost, they would not be alive today. God doesn't give up on us. Are we able to hold out hope to hear from God, even when we struggle to hear a faint whisper of God's voice?

Are we willing to continue to seek? To listen?

Collective Hearing

I once cut my wedding dress to pieces. No, I wasn't going through a bad breakup, or regretting money spent on a one-time garment. I took this dress that is a treasure to me, a treasure from one of the most wonderful days of my life, and repurposed it into something new and needed. Why would I do this?

I used the fabric to sew burial gowns for babies. When our baby girl left us all those years ago, we immediately sought out support, and I, in my typically methodical, research-y, list-making, way of coping, did some research online. I found a local support group for women who had lost children. We met, and talked, and cried, and began walking through the steps of living as a mother with a child lost to miscarriage, stillbirth, or infant death. We walked together to raise money to fight the medical causes of some of our losses, through the March of Dimes. Some of our group taught doctors and nurses how to help parents when they find themselves on this unexpected journey. Others of our group took on special projects that helped bereaved parents. We supported the group and each other through art projects, annual memorial services, and sponsoring bricks for a special memorial garden.

I was busy with my work and my dissertation, so it was rare that I had time to participate in any of these efforts, although I contributed how I could. I felt disconnected due to that busy schedule, but I never stopped listening to what work God might have for me in the group. And then one day, someone emailed with an idea. An idea for sewing wedding gowns into burial gowns. And that is where I heard the still small voice of God, saying. THIS. This is where you can contribute. You have the raw material; you have the skills. Go. Do.

But this is what we do, isn't it? When faced with events that shake us to our core, these earthquakes of loss in our lives, we find community, we support the community, and then we listen for God's still small voice, seeking our call from God, our purpose for the way forward.

For we *are* new. There is no going back to before a big change. There is no un-becoming:

- a parent who has lost a child
- someone who has been fired or downsized
- a person who has survived life-threatening illness
- a lover or friend who has lost the object of their love.

We are forever changed, but must go forward anyway. And God is right there with us when we do.

Listening, Alone and Together

Back to my wedding dress. It was hard to cut it up. It hurt. Although it was only polyester, only cost a few hundred dollars, it was so difficult to deconstruct this artifact of a beautiful memory. But in doing so, I was able to create new things, needed things. And in my loss experience, I had to take apart my previous self. But in doing so, I was able to hear God's voice in new ways, find new callings, new creativity in my life of following God. I was able to do these things because I found, in my support group and in my family and friends, people who were Jesus to me. Being community in their brokenness, coming together to help heal each others' wounds, but most importantly, showing how to go forward, hearing God's call in my life in that time of grief.

We all walk through lives filled with inevitable earthquakes of loss. Only sometimes, we forget to walk together. We must not hide these struggles from each other as we work to discern what is next for us. We can hear God's voice in new ways, and help others hear God's voice, even when it is small, still, and unfamiliar. We can do this by forgoing isolation, by refusing to hide in our personal deserts of grief, and offering invitations. By forgoing fear of the future, and offering community. By forgoing the temptation to hide our struggles, and gathering with open hearts around a welcome table. And by forgoing staying stuck in the rubble, and really listening for God's still small voice calling us to live new lives.

I know you will hear that voice calling you toward your future.

Once you begin to hear that new direction, be your own evangelist and enthusiast. Put up a banner or poster in your home to keep your focus on the future. Post on social media so those who follow you from afar can share in the experience of your transition. Ask a friend to be your personal cheerleader and pep-talk provider for your new direction.

Reflection Questions:

When do you do your best listening to spirit?

When have you heard a call toward a certain direction in the past? What was that experience like for you? What action did you take or not take in response?

~ 8 ~

INTERLUDE: PRACTICES

Transformation is possible in every transition. However, too often, we grapple with these changes without support or guidance, and too often, are left unchanged or changed in negative ways by those experiences. The following practices: acceptance, mindfulness, and sabbath, can be greatly helpful in times of great change. It takes accepting the reality of our current situation to begin moving through it. Mindfulness can help us find a quiet center to anchor us when the world feels unsteady. It can also help us know ourselves and discern a path forward. Sabbath can help us stop everything for at least a short period in order to make room for all these approaches and practices. I hope you'll try on at least one of these practices the next time you are facing a big change

~ 9 ~

ACCEPTANCE

It turns out that radical change is easier to accept than incremental change. People who are asked to make minor changes in their diet and exercise soon slip back into old habits, even if they have had a heart attack and been told these changes are essential to their survival. People who are asked and supported in changing their entire lifestyle after a heart attack have a high success rate, compared to those who tried minor changes who were only half as successful at avoiding future cardiac events (Ornish, 1998).

And yet, we find ourselves needing to accept all kinds of changes, from the minute to the monumental.

Radical Acceptance?

To accept where we are, we may have to let go of our ideas about where we should be. Radical acceptance is an approach that promotes using acceptance to ease our relationship with change. Although the roots of Radical Acceptance come from Buddhism and psychology, there are many ways in which this concept resonates with a Christian faith. First, it echoes the idea that God loves us just as we are right now. The world is not as it should be but is loved and accepted as it is. Second, we hear in scripture to "Be still and know that I am God." This is often used as a meditation or prayer and can be a powerful touchstone for the power of remaining still and accepting the reality of our lives before taking further action. Tara Brach, in her book *Radical Acceptance* (2003), suggests practices for groups or individuals that can help with learning this practice. These include quiet periods of guided reflection and meditation. Some echo ancient prayer practices rooted in the Christian tradition. Spiritual direction often includes learning to radically accept one's place on their spiritual path before taking steps in any forward direction.

Boats and Blinding Lights

At various times the disciples had to accept that nothing would ever be the same, going forward into terrifying new paths, leaving their old lives completely behind. Peter, who seemed to make a career out of missing the point of Jesus even as he followed him, and not the bravest of all individuals, is called by the risen Christ to go forth and feed His sheep, after being so terrified by the sight of him he jumps off a boat (John 21:7). Paul, a guy who loved to go to extremes, is struck blind before being called out of his old life of terrorizing and oppressing religious minorities into a new life of spreading the good news of radical love through evangelism and planting churches (Acts 9).

We may have more in common with Peter and Paul than we want to acknowledge. We are terrified and want to run away in the face of change. Paul's way of being in the world was deeply rooted in his own personal struggles. His extremist nature (which, unfortunately, he carried into some of his Christian theology) may have been the natural response of someone in a deeply unsettling context seeking something solid and unyielding to grasp, for safety, for stability. Yet even with all this baggage, which might keep others from making any change at all, Peter and Paul were able to take their transformative experiences and radically change direction.

The Things We Carry

We too often have a great deal of baggage. Some primal wounds perhaps, or just the unsettledness of modern life with its accompanying stress and emotional strains. And it is okay to be exactly who we are—broken and beautiful and complex! Our emotional stuff, though, may be holding us back, holding us in place. Our emotional stuff, more than the heavy relational work and personal burdens we may be bearing, can make our load feel unbearable. We feel so weary we can barely move, much less step out on faith. How can we start moving forward without such unnecessary stuff?

What are you struggling to accept? The reality of your situation? Your own inner gifts? The challenges facing you internally or externally?

By accepting where you are and letting go of those things that are holding you back, you can live into the amazing, powerful, shining life God has placed within us. You can begin this day to liberate yourselves and all those you encounter, by truly letting go.

Reflection Questions:

What might it shift if you cultivated radical acceptance?

What do you need to accept make your load lighter as you travel through change? What do you need help carrying? What do you need to lay down?

~ 10 ~

MINDFULNESS

The roots of mindfulness are often traced in origin to Eastern Philosophies. However, mindfulness is a part of almost every faith tradition in one way or another. Although practically ignored for many centuries in Christian tradition, mindfulness through contemplative prayer and meditation has also been a part of Christianity since its beginnings. Ancient church fathers and mothers spent hours in prayer and meditation in hopes of finding God's spirit within themselves, retreating to caves or deserts in pursuit of the elusive essence of faith. Many modern churches have begun to have regular opportunities for such prayer or meditation, including practicing Lectio Divina, centering prayer, body prayer, and other prayer practices that increase mindfulness of self and faith. If you struggle with getting started on mindfulness, churches, meditation centers and/or individual teachers trained in some or all these practices of mindfulness can help you learn how to practice them.

Practice Makes Perfect

Developing a practice of mindfulness or meditation is another way we can increase our capacity for acceptance. Mindfulness is the practice of being aware of our experiences in the moment without judging those experiences.

Research shows that we can increase our mindfulness abilities through regular and intentional practice (Hofmann and Gómez, 2017). Increasing our mindfulness changes our brain patterns in ways that can be measured through brain scanning. It concretely transforms our neural responses. This change in neural responses reduces our emotional reactivity, increases our skills for flexible thinking, and dampens those brain reactions to unexpected events which keep us off balance and unable to move forward (Taylor, et al., 2011).

When Jesus was facing transitions in his life and ministry, he withdrew for times of prayer, away from the crowds. This can serve as an example for us to take time for mindfulness when change seems all around us.

Expect the Unexpected

For me, the more tumultuous life gets, the harder it is to stay mindful. I am reminded of a favorite story of hearing God in unexpected places in the face of loss and fear. This tale from Acts 16 also includes a literal earthquake, and is a powerful reminder of the power of listening for God in times of intense shock and stress.

After suffering the great loss of their master, their rabbi, their friend, the disciples do continue in community and carry their calling forward. Soon enough, Paul and Silas have been jailed for their teaching and healing in the name of Jesus. Suddenly there was an earthquake, so violent that the foundations of the prison were shaken; and immediately all the doors were opened and everyone's chains were unfastened. When the jailer woke up and saw the prison doors thrown open, he drew his sword and was about to kill himself, since he supposed that the prisoners had escaped. But Paul shouted in a loud voice, "Do not harm yourself, for we are all here." The jailer called for lights, and rushing in, he fell down trembling before Paul and Silas. Then he brought them out. They spoke the word of the Lord to him and to all who were in his house. At the same hour of the night, he took them and washed their wounds, then he and his entire family were baptized without delay. He brought them up into the house and set food before them. He and his entire household rejoiced.

A literal earthquake is shaking the jail in which they are held for continuing to teach and heal in the name of Jesus. Their bonds are broken, the doors thrown wide. They are free! But instead of the story continuing with the cells being empty, clear evidence of the miracle that had occurred, the disciples have remained. They have remained to reassure and aid the jailer. The jailer, who believed all was lost, was considering suicide rather than taking the harsh punishment due him from authorities had he failed in his duties. Like Elijah, he would rather die than face what he believes the future holds. But the disciples, through extending their community to him, inspire him to join with them as he is still reeling from this earthquake experience. And in joining them, he finds his mission to go forward, hosting and healing and celebrating the Disciples while leading others to God.

There may be times when we feel we can't hear a word God is saying for us. And that is completely normal. Even Mother Theresa testifies to having years of her life when she struggled to hear God's voice in the way she was accustomed. When we can't hear God in our usual ways, we must remember to listen. God's voice can come to us in most unexpected ways. For when God isn't heard in the loud wind or earthquake or fire, God can be heard in the silent stillness. And when God can't be heard over our grief and fears and hopelessness, God can be heard in the fellowship and care of our community.

Practicing Mindfulness

While I am no expert, I have found a few things helpful for mindfulness in my own life. Spending time in nature, noticing everything I can see or hear at that moment, teaches me about being present. Standing with bare feet or just laying on the ground literally grounds me, connects me to something solid and larger than myself. Practicing guided meditations recorded by others when I can't deal with silence trains me to focus my attention and listen. Then, when I am ready for silence, I have some of the tools I need to keep me listening rather than getting distracted.

You may have mindfulness practices that have worked well for you in the past. There are a surplus of traditions and teachers you can use to find the right ones for you. If mindfulness is new to you, I suggest just trying a few, maybe the ones I listed above. It can be so challenging to stay mindful during times of change, so having a few trusted practices to rely on can help you when the storm of change seems to rage all around.

Reflection Questions:

Have you ever tried a mindfulness practice, individually or in a group? How was that experience for you?

When have you felt centered and grounded enough to sit in silence with only your thoughts? What were you doing at the time? How can you find more times like that?

~ 11 ~

SABBATH

You are most likely to learn from change when you take time to process the experience. On a personal level, this means:

- Feeling the ending.
- Refusing to rush the middle.
- Planning for the new beginning.

As William Bridges (1991) highlighted in his groundbreaking works on life transitions, when we do not appreciate the need to fully experience and process every aspect of a life change or transition, we are likely to rush through it and be discouraged if we can't do so. We may feel confused, disoriented, and want to rush through or abandon the situation. But we lose much opportunity when we try to rush transitions. Especially when we do not take time to leverage the in-between times. Bridges describes this in-between time as a neutral zone, and explains, "Painful though it often is, the neutral zone is the individuals and the organization's best chance for creativity, renewal, and development."

Time and Transformation
Jesus went into the desert for 40 days and fasted and prayed before beginning his public ministry (Luke 4). He honored the need to

process this change in direction, before embarking on a new way of being in the world.

Being intentional about time to process transitions means having a game plan long before a big change takes place. This can be as simple as building in time to journal or talk to friends. A member of a church experiencing a pastoral transition, Christine, explained how talking to other church members helped build a sense of love and reassurance during a change in pastors. "You always have close friends, and they're the ones you talked to..., that's who your friends are. I guess we had to reassure each other, and there's more people doing the reassuring than there were people that were really uptight about it."

Even if a change is fast, you can find time to sit with it and process. Remember, Jesus only had 40 days to have some profound spiritual experiences, and you can do the same in the time you have. We can find the pause in the midst of change. There is an old parable told by the Taoist Liu An in *Huainanzi* (2010), that I like to tell in this way:

There was once a farmer who lost his horse. He tried, but could not find and catch him. His neighbors were very concerned, exclaiming, "How bad for you!"

The farmer pondered this and said, "Bad or good, too soon to tell."

The horse came back with a mare it had found to be its mate. His neighbors were overjoyed, exclaiming, "How good for you!"

The farmer pondered this and said, "Good or bad, too soon to tell."

The farmer's son was riding the new horse and broke his leg. His neighbors were again very concerned, exclaiming, "How bad for you!"

The farmer pondered this and said, "Bad or good, too soon to tell."

Very soon after that there came a war. All of the young men who were able went to fight. But the son's broken leg kept him at home. His neighbors were weeping for their own sons, gone to war, and said to the farmer, "How good for you that your son does not have to go and fight."

Once again, the farmer pondered all that had happened and said, "Bad or good, too soon to tell."

It can be almost impossible to stop and reserve judgment about unexpected change. But as we see in this parable, it is impossible to know the full consequences of something unexpected until we get much further down the road. The challenge of big changes is that our own judgments and the judgments of others cloud our ability to find the right path through change or find those areas where we can take back some control through acceptance, action, or ritual. Yet we must push through our unhelpful brain reactions toward just those things. Unexpected and seemingly random change is in fact embedded in living as human beings, despite our perceptions of control and predictability. And if we do recognize that our pursuits of control may keep us from God's calling, what practices can truly help us let go?

Planting Seeds and Waiting

In thinking about taking time and letting go of control, I can't help but think about our garden. I have a love hate relationship with it most of the time. I love the food we grow. Yet I hate the mess. I hate the weeds. And I love sitting on my porch looking at the leaves and blooms filling our yard with color. See, the problem is, gardening takes patience. I don't have a lot of it. See my previous comments about always being ready for this "life stuff" to be over so things can get back to normal. Well that's the funny thing about gardening. Normal is all the phases of growing. Normal is digging up dirt. Normal is paying money for poop and then spreading it to enrich the soil. Normal is planting seeds in nice neat rows. Normal is when those nice neat rows grow up all crazy with plants entangled with weeds fed with the aforementioned poop. Normal is pulling weeds and watching new ones spring up the next day. Normal is beautiful flowers that blossom just as you had planned. Normal is some plants that die before blooming. Normal is eating delicious meals grown by your own labor. Normal is turning those plants under to get ready to start again next season. Guess what else is like that?

The wisdom of the garden says that life, that God's light, that Word, is always present no matter how dark and cold the winter gets. The weather says...stay inside. The garden says...come outside and get ready. The season says...nothing can grow. The garden says...trust your seeds and bulbs to grow. The world says...what light? God says...the light is always within you, whether you can recognize and believe it.

A few years ago, Amy Grant, one of my favorite singers from my junior high years, wrote a song about life inspired by an orchard, called "Better Not to Know." In it, she sings about the great unknown of sowing seeds, and living life, and loving others without being certain of the outcome.

In the end, we're all gardeners, all farmers, trying to tend this seed of light that has been planted within us since the beginning. We don't know how it will grow, which plants will thrive and which will die. We have to let go of control, to wait to find out in time.

Taking Sabbath

One practical way to learn to let go of control is to practice Sabbath. Sabbath, in ancient Israel, was both the practice of resting one day a week but also practices of letting land rest, forgiving debts, and acting in sustainable ways with others in the community. The word sustainable is key here. Pauses like the practice of Sabbath cushion change in ways that make our lives more sustainable.

Ross L. Smillie (2011) observes that modern Sabbath observance can serve as a formative practice when people and communities remember to think beyond economics, marketing, social pressures, consumption, and frantic activity as indicators of success. Time away from this pressure shows that other ways of living are not only possible but joyful, life-giving, and desirable.

When do you take time to pause its activity to rest and imagine alternatives? I challenge you to find a week very soon where you can pause, halting all normal activities for a time of prayer and rest. For smaller pauses, build short times of silence and reflection into your daily routine. You might be surprised by the possibilities you find in your imagination when activity slows down a bit.

Reflection Questions:

What is your favorite Bible Study about change?

Have you tried a Sabbath practice when dealing with changes in your life? What was that like?

When do you take time to pause your activity to rest?

~ 12 ~

INTERLUDE: CHALLENGES AND CONSIDERATIONS

When going through a change, unexpected or not, deeper challenges can threaten to sabotage our learning and sidetrack our progress. If we fail to acknowledge grief that is often present in times of change, we can get stuck. The truism about grief, that the only way past it is through it, applies also in times of life change. We can feel shame when experiencing loss or change, and processing feelings of shame in healthy ways can be especially tricky. Both community and family can be our biggest assets when working through change but can also be challenging. Those in our lives can be challenged when we change, especially if it changes the way we interact with or support them. The following chapters contain insights and strategies that may help you with the grief, shame, community and family dimensions of change.

~ 13 ~

GRIEF

While transitions can bring gifts, they can also bring challenges and pain. They often bring grief, and hard goodbyes. Before we can travel any new roads, we must first honor the emotional and practical need to say goodbye.

Hard Goodbyes

I know a few things about saying goodbye.

I have said goodbye to many jobs and homes over the years, some I loved, some I didn't. I have lost two college roommates far too young, one inexplicably just after she moved back home from college and one just a few years ago after a lifelong battle with depression. Because of my blended family, I have lost 7 grandparents, in some cases with much preparation and lengthy chances for closure, in other cases their death came suddenly and shocked us all.

In the years since we lost our daughter Millie, we have unsuccessfully tried to adopt privately and from foster care, and did not receive a placement before our finances and our emotional well-being made moving forward impossible. Finally, we said goodbye to our dream of having children grow up in our home.

Recently, two churches I got to know over the past few years had their final worship services. The decisions to end their worshiping life together came out of deep discernment over their future after their numbers shrank and their ability to do ministry waned. They navigated change into a new direction, sure, but it was a direction that came with much grief and pain as they celebrated the beautiful gifts these congregations shared with their members and communities over their lives. Another church I was working with walked with a pastor through a serious illness and death, and this had long-lasting and profound effects on their life together.

Every one of these goodbyes was a heartbreak. Some broke my heart into so many pieces I thought I'd never put them back together again. But here I am. Maybe not as together as I once was, but a whole person knit together from the broken pieces.

I am sure you have had losses too, and hard goodbyes, and lessons I know you could share. Endings are one of the hardest and most inevitable parts of being alive. Forrest Church (2008) says:

> Love is grief's advance party. ...Every time we give our heart away, we risk having it dashed to pieces. Fear promises a safer path: refuse to give away your heart and it will never be broken. And it is true, armored hearts are invulnerable. We can eliminate a world of trouble from our lives simply by closing our hearts. Yet the trouble from which we are liberating ourselves is necessary trouble. We need it as we need breath. Since the most precious and enduring lifework is signed by love, to avoid the risk of love is to cower from life's only perfect promise. (Church, 2008, p. 57)

So what can we do when we must navigate these inevitable rapids of loss? I had the same question, every time I found myself there.

The Work of Grief

Since I am a researcher, you may not be surprised to hear how, when faced with Millie's death, one of the first things I did was check out some books on how to cope with the loss of a child from our local library. I found some wisdom that helped me heal there, which I have used and will carry with me the rest of my life. In my research, I found some amazing advice for those of us who are saying goodbye, to a loved one, to a stage of life or a long-held dream. The biggest thing I learned was that grieving, saying goodbye, is a work that we must do. We must go through it, we can't go around it or skip it, and if we try, it will come back around and meet us there.

In practical terms, there are a few steps that were helpful to me in saying my goodbyes. Maybe some of these can be gifts to you as they have been to me:

Take care of yourself. You are recovering from a soul injury when you are saying goodbye, which requires at least as much care as a physical wound. Feed yourself well. Let others feed you if that's what it takes. Take yourself out in the fresh air daily. Go slow with returning to non-essential responsibilities. Experiment with healing practices such as massage, reiki, meditation. Find the practices that feed you and keep going. reiki wasn't for me, but meditation was. And massage, the feeling of being touched and held was a revelation.

Give yourself time and space to be sad, mad, relieved, anxious, or have whatever feelings you have. There are no wrong feelings when saying a big goodbye. If anyone tells you that there are, put them in their place and get back to your healing work. If reading about the common stages of grief is helpful, use it. If your experience is nothing like that, don't worry. We are people, not processes. It looks different for everyone.

For me, I found reading the Psalms profound. From them I heard words like:

I grow weary because of my groaning: every night I drench my bed and flood my couch with tears.

My eyes are wasted with grief.

My days drift away like smoke: and my bones are hot as burning coals.

My heart is smitten like grass and withered: so that I forget to eat my bread.

The chords of death entangled me; the grip of the grave took hold of me: I came to grief and sorrow.

My eye is consumed with sorrow, and also my throat and my belly. For my life is wasted with grief, and my years with sighing.

The raw language of anguish and grief from thousands of years ago made me feel less alone in my suffering, and reminded me that as humans, we have always grieved and will always grieve.

Find ways to remember and give thanks for whatever you have lost. Telling stories with others who know and understand is a long-held tradition in my family over meals after funerals. After Millie, journaling my memories of her short life with us was healing for me. Art can be another way to remember and be thankful, whether creating a scrapbook of memories or creating a work of art to capture your feelings about the loss. A memory object, or small shrine with items that are meaningful, can be a literal touchstone to help us carry that which we have lost along on our journey. I have had several little altars throughout the last few years.

Also don't forget to tell the stories of what is left behind: strong, resilient people who can and will go on. People that are necessary to the future we need in this world. Do this in community when you can.

A Long and Winding Road

Allow time and memory to play their games. If one day, you feel as though it has been a while since you remember feeling devastated to the point of weeping, that's a good thing. And if another day, you are sitting in the tub and begin crying uncontrollably at a memory that surges into your mind from the past, that's a good thing as well. None of this is linear, all of this is cyclical, but regardless, we will all walk into our future, one step at a time.

Say goodbye to your old self. As we say goodbye to that self, which is shaped and informed by our past and our culture, we will go through grief and frightening liminal spaces. But then we can open our eyes, slowly and sometimes falteringly, to see what God loves about us and others beyond those old ideas of self. We can become more forgiving and giving, and more open and direct. We can grow confident that the time we have, however fleeting, is good, and more awaits us across a horizon we must only trust.

The true gift of all this is, once we work through these patterns of a healthy goodbye, they will be with us forever. We may forget, but when we again experience great loss, our emotional muscle memory may just remember. It did for me. When I realized recently that I had to grieve the loss of a stage of my life just as I had grieved those people I had lost in the past, I began with self-care. I honored my memories and gave thanks for those experiences I had along the way. I remembered my resilience and how I did have a future, even if not the one I imagined.

Only after a good goodbye can we turn our attention to the future. A future that will involve more goodbyes, to be sure, but also many joyful hellos.

Reflection Questions:

What do you do when you are grieving? What has been most helpful and meaningful?

What do you need to grieve about a change you are facing? How will you do this grief work?

~ 14 ~

SHAME

Change too often brings us a feeling of shame. Perhaps we weren't successful at something hoped for, a job ended before we were ready, or real or imagined judgments on a romantic or family situation hurt and worry us. We can't navigate change successfully without facing our shame.

Shame into Praise?

Zephaniah was a prophet who was living through a time of great change and transition in the kingdom of Israel, centuries before the birth of Jesus. A time when God is speaking through oracles and prophets to call Israel to task over their sins and complacency. Zephaniah responds by anticipating the in-breaking of God to set things right. For the most part, his visions and those of the oracles focused on the devastation they believe God will bring to the community. Scholars believe much of these writings were from a time after Israel was exiled, so truthfully, these predictions echoed the already existing feeling in Israel of being cast out, punished with defeat, failure, and shame in the eyes of other nations. Yet after passage upon passage describing the harsh judgment of God on Israel's people, we hear Zephaniah say:

> *Sing aloud, O daughter Zion; shout, O Israel! Rejoice and exult with all your heart, O daughter Jerusalem! The Lord has taken away the judgments against you, he has turned away your enemies. The king of Israel, the Lord, is in your midst; you shall fear disaster no more. On that day it shall be said to Jerusalem: Do not fear, O Zion; do not let your hands grow weak. The Lord, your God, is in your midst, a warrior who gives victory; he will rejoice over you with gladness, he will renew you in his love; he will exult over you with loud singing as on a day of festival. I will remove disaster from you, so that you will not bear reproach for it. I will deal with all your oppressors at that time. And I will save the lame and gather the outcast, and I will change their shame into praise.* (Zephaniah 3:14-19)

The book of Zephaniah thus becomes almost a drama, one that prophetically and ritually traces the fall of Israel and now points to its redemption. While all this history is fascinating, what really got me about this passage were two phrases and the questions they awoke in me: How can shame become praise? And, how can we truly fear disaster no more?

Shame and Grief

Shame, as explained by Brene Brown in *Braving the Wilderness* (2017), is at its essence the fear of disconnection. So where does this fear, this shame, originate?

We feel shame when we fail or perceive a change as failure. Too often this shame is the sharpest with visible failures such as the loss of a home or business, a failed relationship, or a desired award or promotion that passes us by. But we may also feel shame at our failures to live up to who we feel we should be. These shoulds are sometimes good things, as when we strive to become more loving, more giving, more connected. Other times the shoulds are shaped by society, as in how we should live, consume, look, work and act. In either case, shame can creep in, and while failures to live up to worthy goals of love and generosity should be teaching moments for us, shame, or the fear of being disconnected from love, tends to be less helpful and in fact, increases the likelihood of our separation or isolation from our communities and our God.

Grief can also bring shame alongside. When we lose someone or something we love, or lose independence, or good health, we can feel ashamed we are mortal. That we loved those who are mortal. We can feel ashamed we are not super humans or robots. Shouldn't we have had it so together that none of this would have happened to us? Doesn't everyone else seem to have it together? It can feel shameful to suffer loss. We are embarrassed to grieve rather than put on a happy face for everyone. We are ashamed if we are still grieving after what we perceive or have heard is too long. We are embarrassed by the fact we have thought that others might be grieving too long in the past.

We feel thrown if we are now the ones going through exactly what we always said we could never make it through. We are scared these losses will be seen as something that could contaminate others and drive them away in fear. We can find ourselves ashamed and humiliated by our very nerve to be human beings, rather than humbled by the wonder of how every human, so many humans, will suffer loss and they will grieve, and yet they will wake up, and they will keep going and keep loving.

Now shame is a natural part of the cycle of grief, whether grieving a personal failure or profound loss. I can testify there were deep feelings of shame in me after we lost our daughter. I don't know where these feelings came from, exactly, but I felt a sense of failure of our fertility journey when it ended this way, and also a sense of being an inconvenience to all those who heard about my loss, a shadow creeping across the sun of their happy world, their own worst case scenario come to life. I expended way too much effort trying to appear "normal" so I would not be a human reminder of the tragic vulnerability of babies in our modern and medical world. But while shame is now understood as a natural part of grieving, I would argue it is not a highly helpful part of grief or any other experience. Because, ironically, feeling shame often causes us to self-isolate, bringing about the very disconnection we fear most.

Failures and Fears

Feelings of shame around failure or loss don't arise in a vacuum, either. There is great stigma in our culture around weakness, around vulnerability, around getting sick, or experiencing loss, or failing at anything at all. This stigma persists even though every single human will experience all these things at one point or another.

On a more personal level, shame correlates what many of us fear: losing control (or the illusion of it), the shift of our sense of self from triumphant to tragic, being dependent on others and fearing they will find us such a burden, feeling abandoned and lost.

Yet I don't want to leave the impression shame is only found in times of failure and grief. Due to childhood events or past hurts, we can often internalize a sense of shame which is less correlated with a particular situation or event. Regardless of where we get it, though, shame whispers in our ears, "If others only knew, they would stay as far away from us as possible." Knew what? If they knew who we really are, because we are clearly not good enough.

I frequently spend time with Brene Brown's work on shame and vulnerability, which I referenced above. Brown (2017) says that in her years of interviewing people about connection and love, she heard story after story about shame. And she connected the dots to realize: shame exists because we feel terribly vulnerable, vulnerable to isolation, shunning, abandonment, disconnection in all its forms.

Richard Rohr (2016) writes about how we can read Jesus' encounters with the disciples, and particularly his instructions to the disciples to go forward without shoes or belongings, as initiations into a new way, a way of vulnerability, which will bring about the Kingdom of God. Rohr says, "When read in light of classic initiation patterns, Jesus' intentions are very clear. He wanted his disciples--then and now—to experience the value of vulnerability."

How can we experience this vulnerability, and make it the essence of our Christian path, without slipping into shame?

Dressed for the Occasion

Brene Brown found out in her research that those people who had less shame had a stronger sense of love and belonging and their own worthiness of love. This feeling of worth gave them the courage to be imperfect without shame. They were able to treat themselves and others with kindness. They were able to be their authentic selves. To get all this, what did they have to give up? They had to leave behind a sense of who they thought they should be.

And when the disciples went forth, they had to give up who they thought they should be. Some of them were businessmen, some were fishermen, some were quick to jump into a fight. They became vulnerable by giving up their assets and vocations and their weapons, and even their shoes, to go forth as poor pilgrims in order to change the world.

In our modern world, wanderers and pilgrims might have trouble surviving without shoes. Dusty paths and foot washing have gone extinct in the face of hot pavement and no shoes, no service. But we are given some instructions, or inspiration for a life of vulnerability without shame, in Paul's letter to the Colossians.

> As God's chosen ones, holy and beloved, clothe yourselves with compassion, kindness, humility, meekness, and patience. Bear with one another and, if anyone has a complaint against another, forgive each other; just as the Lord has forgiven you, so you also must forgive. Above all, clothe yourselves with love, which binds everything together in perfect harmony. And let the peace of Christ rule in your hearts, to which indeed you were called in the one body. And be thankful. (Colossians 3:12-17)

So we are going to need to go forth without some of our clothes.

We can take off all our statuses and shoulds and put on compassion for ourselves and others. Compassion starts within, but by practicing it regularly with others, we may find a greater understanding of how everyone fails, everyone suffers loss, everyone grieves. That there is no shame in any of this and that there will be others out there, who, like us, refuse to sever connection just because someone has the nerve to be human.

We can take off judgment and put on kindness, giving ourselves and others grace for failures which might be of our own making. Sometimes we do the wrong thing or make mistakes. Sometimes we pay dearly for them. We are still worthy of love and connection, and so is everyone else.

We can take off fear and put on meekness and humility, understanding that all we have and do are fragile and fleeting and can be gone in a moment. We are not our accomplishments or our possessions. We can live into the belief that there is no shame in having none of either.

We can take off busyness and put on patience. We can be patient with those who are hurting or grieving. We can be patient with our own hurt or grief. Life is not a race to be the fastest to get over something. Life is not a game with end zone of "back to normal." Practicing this patience will equip us to realize there is nothing shameful in being human, even if it means some things take a long and complicated time to resolve.

And most of all, we can take off isolation and put on love. Loving others starts with loving ourselves. We can remember that whether we win or lose, succeed or fail, live up to our or society's shoulds, lose parts of our selves or our hearts or our possessions, we are worthy of love. And remember we are already loved. God goes first in loving us boldly and unconditionally, so we can see the kind of love we are to have for ourselves and others.

Living Without Fear

Now, let's go back to Zephaniah for just a minute and address this question: *How can we be truly free to fear disaster no more?* We, like Israel, may have suffered great setbacks, failures, and trials. We have felt shame at these experiences. And yet, we are called to turn that shame into praise and fear disaster no more. Just loving ourselves and others is not enough, we are called to a life without fear.

I keep going back to the idea of taking off status, possessions, and shoulds. How much fear is tied up in these parts of our lives and our selves? We fear failure, we fear setback, we fear all our efforts will be for naught. But doesn't this again clothe us in external evaluations of who we are, rather than the understanding of how God loves us, God loves us when we fail, God loves us when we suffer loss, God loves us when we are vulnerable enough to open our hearts and risk having them broken. God loves us when we cast aside our fears and give loving a shot, take a chance on risk, try though we know we surely will fail sometimes at some things before it's all over. God is the reason we can fear no more. Because in spite of anything we experience, we are no longer under threat of disconnection from love. God's love is ever present and unchanging, and not going anywhere, even if, like Israel in Zephaniah's time, we lose everything.

Once we get that, once we really get it, then let's take off our status, our shoulds, our fears, our efforts to maintain an image of perfection and invulnerability. Let's put on all our other clothes, of compassion, kindness, meekness, humility, and patience, and get to work loving others. Pushing through fear and reminding ourselves this: If all is lost, we are loved and God is here. Leaning in to love when we and those around us are sad, or shocked, or confused or reeling with loss.

It might not feel natural at first. We have a whole culture sending out the message that everyone is not worthy of love. But the longer we practice loving ourselves the better we will get at loving others. The more we practice living without fear the more we will take the bold steps forward into our futures. And loving others boldly, taking the risk of showing others our true selves, free of the clothes of shame or stigma, can free all those we encounter to do the same.

Reflection Questions:

Where is shame in your experience of change? Which changes in your life have felt like failures? Which have felt like disconnection?

What can you put on and take off to shift your relationship with shame? Who can help you with this work?

~ 15 ~

CHANGE AND YOUR FAMILY LIFE

When we are facing change, our families can be a major factor in how we experience it. Family means different things to different people. In your life, family may include spouses, children, parents and siblings, chosen families of your peers or elders, or some combination of the above. No matter how you define family, you will need their support or at least lack of resistance if you seek a healthy relationship with change.

With fellow adults, I might encourage sharing this book with them, so they might also work on change readiness. There are also a few strategies you can use to help them join you on your journey if they have their own complicated relationship with change. With children, there are some practical approaches which can help, especially if the change is impacting their lives as well. Let's start there.

In some ways, children can seem more adaptable than adults. They experience change every year when they transition from one grade or school to the next. Many children find their families changing through the addition of siblings or parental divorce or marriage. Others move across states and countries as their parents take new jobs or return to school.

In other ways, though, children are supported by routines. So anything that changes those routines can be challenging. Just as with adults, this can become an opportunity to help children build skills for transition and change that will help them throughout their lives.

What practices are most helpful for teaching children about transition and change?

Talking about Change with Children and Teens

Explain things truthfully in a way children can understand. Depending on their age, they may become aware fairly quickly from adult conversations and behavior that something big is going on. Tell them what is happening. Explain that change is a normal part of life. Explain what parts of life will continue as normal, and which may change. Allow ample time for questions they may have.

Acknowledge their feelings, using their own language to help them process the experience. Do not use language which negates their feelings, like "Don't be sad," or, "Let's just don't think about that."

When you answer their questions, do so in an age-appropriate manner. Even if you try to explain the change to them on their level, they are likely overhearing things you may need to explain more fully. Try to keep explanations simple and age-appropriate so children can understand. Reassure them that when things seem confusing or scary, God is with all of us.

Listen to young people about what they would like to see come out of the change. Let their answers be as silly or serious as needed. Talk about how you might work together to make those dreams that are possible a reality. The wisdom of children can also give us insights we may not otherwise find.

Use stories of change in the Bible as a jumping off point for talking about change. The stories of Joseph's life, or the stories of Mary facing her unexpected role in God's story, can be helpful in understanding where God is in times of change.

Share prayer practices which go beyond simply talking to God. Embodied prayer, such as walking prayers or movement prayers, or labyrinth walking, can be a way of praying during changes that take away our words for what is happening to us.

Discuss the way creation illustrates the power of change. Examples might include a river changing course, a caterpillar turning to a butterfly, or the evolution of a plant or animal species over time. God is in these natural wonders even as they change. Have the students share their favorite story of change from the natural world.

Use the Gospels to discuss how Jesus' ministry changed over time. What did he do differently as he spent longer in ministry? Did Jesus change his mind? (The story of the Syro-Phoenician woman in Mark 7:24-30 could be helpful here.) How can we learn from Jesus' example of listening to God about when change is needed?

Practice Listening Together

The most transformative experiences are often those where ample opportunities are provided for reflection and peer support. Try the following:

Ask children and teenagers what changes they have experienced/are experiencing in their lives. Have them explain what has helped them cope with change in the past so they can learn from their own experiences.

Have each child write a letter to God about a change they are struggling with. Use a few Psalms as examples of how the Psalmists both praised God and expressed their anger and questions to God. If they are comfortable, have them share their letters with the family. Close by praying for each other's struggles and celebrations around their change.

Ask teenagers or young adults in the family to support younger family members who will soon go through what they have experienced on the journey from childhood to young adulthood. What lessons would they share?

With the addition of these thoughtful tools and practices, children and teenagers can be supported and enriched in their spiritual path during times of transition.

Can't We All Be Adults about This?

In terms of the adults in your family and friend networks, the same principles can apply, if implemented a little differently. Talk with the adults you are close with about what you are going through. Be upfront about what may change for them as things change for you. Listen to their feelings but maintain healthy boundaries about your own centrality in the change. Encourage them to find other listening ears outside the situation as needed. Include them in your storytelling, practices, rituals, and celebrations. Let them add their own elements when appropriate to process any losses they may be feeling. Invite everyone involved to reflect regularly on the process of change through journaling or spiritual practices. When you are ready, share conversations on what you are all learning during this time of change. If you get stuck in terms of family reactions to change, family counseling can provide a neutral space to explore how best to support each other during this time.

Reflection Questions:

How did your family of origin approach change? How do you approach it with your current family?

What changes might those in your family be dealing with in their own lives?

What activities would you like to try to facilitate learning from change among your family members?

~ 16 ~

COMMUNITY

As we have seen, change can leave us shocked, confused and feeling lost, just like the disciples after the crucifixion of Jesus. The fantastic news is that learning during experiences of change and transition can help us develop change skills we can use going forward. We can become better equipped to handle transition and change and learn from those experiences whenever we encounter them (Alonderiene and Pundziene, 2008). All this effort is worth it, not only for any particular transition you may be facing this year, but for all life's changes facing you in the years to come. With the knowledge of Jesus' call toward transformation, an understanding of the need to open or change our minds, and a loving community for support, we can find new understanding on the other side of whatever unexpected change comes our way.

Practice Reflection with Others
Transformative learning requires critical reflection. We learn best when we reflect on how change intersects our ideas, beliefs, and frames of reference. We can critically examine the new ideas our experience is forming in us and avoid simply shoring up what we already believe. We can keep an eye out for points at which our new experiences might be showing us a new way of thinking. We can stay open to changing our beliefs and ideas. We can take notes,

so we can process all these reflections, or talk about them with others.

We know a few things from research about how to do this sort of critical reflection in groups. Transformative learning in groups most often results from high stakes events and working on meaningful problems together (Watkins and Marsick, 2010; Ziegler, 1999). One man I interviewed, Ted, remembered a transformational experience serving on a pastoral search committee.

> *Through this, especially there toward the end, we talked a lot about clarity and discerning God's will. We said ...this trite thing that every pastor search committee everywhere says. 'We know God's already picked this person out. We've just got to find the person.' It is trite but it is also very true. We knew that God wasn't going to gift wrap this and say, 'Here he is.' Although, it was almost that way.... it was one of the clearest times of my life of seeing God's will manifested. There have been some other times in other situations down through the years, but that was a very clear time.... I consider that part of the God work. Where God helps make things happen. I don't think God ever forces anything, I think that goes against His nature, the way He chooses to deal with us, but He certainly put those pieces in place.*

It is possible Ted could have drawn these conclusions on his own, but conversation with other committee members about the role of God and the role of their work in the future of the congregation framed the eventual outcome as "God work" for him.

This type of collective reflection is not easy work, and it takes collaboration, trust, and honesty to attempt it. Do you have a community where you feel safe enough when thinking "you know, I thought one thing was true, but I am realizing I was wrong" to say those words out loud? A community where you can feel held enough to stay in the discomfort of change long enough to pass through it to the other side? Finding people who can help you learn and grow from change is key to transformation, and a worthwhile quest whether or not you are not facing big changes in your life.

Support One Another

To avoid resistance or getting stuck in times of change, we must build support systems to carry us through. We sometimes hear negative messages about change from our peers, implying change is bad and means either hard work ahead or is a sign of failure or defeat. Unexpected change is frequently seen by us and by others as bad news. It can be hard to share an unexpected change with those in our lives because we fear their reaction. Often these changes are quite tangled up with our shame that things are not rolling along as planned for us anymore. Others' reactions, no matter how well-meaning, can serve to reinforce this shame. People seek to help us figure out where we went wrong or tell us stories of worse things that happened to them or someone they knew.

We are not unique in experiencing unhelpful friends and family during times of change. In the biblical story of Job, after he loses his wealth, his family, and his health, friends ask him if he deserved all this for something bad he had done, ask him if he could stop dwelling on his misfortune, and ask him how he could be so greedy as to want all his wealth back (Job 4, 8, 11).

How many of us have heard reactions like this from friends and family when dealing with an unexpected life change? All this is grounded in labeling the event as "bad news." Yet we never really know what will come from a change.

Build Change Skills into Community

Once we use tools like reflection, mindfulness, and ritual to accept our new direction, then what? Community can support us through change, and in times of transitions affecting the whole community, can be invaluable for our transformation.

What if every person experiencing a profound change had a community of support and guidance so that through this experience, they might be transformed for the better? We might find ourselves more receptive and optimistic in times of change, knowing our community had our back. We might rest in the knowledge and hope that change is necessary to help us become all we were created to be. What a wonderful possibility!

With our community, we can take a fearless inventory of our own calls from God and the internal and external resources which will be most helpful for our new journey. Then, we can begin noticing what gifts, talents, and resources are present in our community, and ask one another if we are willing to share. What do we each need for this change that we do not possess? Who has this gift, or passion, or knowledge? How can we ask them for it?

This asking can be the most difficult step of all. If we needed a European power adapter for a trip overseas, we might not hesitate to ask a friend who had recently been to Europe. But if we need to borrow some resilience, or some positive attitude, or help navigating the job market, we often forget to ask for just what we need. Often all we need to do is ask to get what we need, and as a bonus, this strengthens our relationships and support systems.

We need support and companions on our journeys. These relationships and connections will sustain us when our new road is long and exhausting.

Use Change to Find Where We Belong

Australian Eddie Kneebone explained how his Aboriginal people made youth feel important and feel that they belonged to the community (Hammond, 1995). They would share a secret piece of knowledge that could ensure the tribe's survival, such as information about a medicinal plant or a source of fresh water. This made the young people feel that they had a vital role to play in the community, that the community could not live without their gifts.

Belonging is essential for our humanity. When we have it, we are healthier, happier, and more likely to have a positive impact on our world. When we don't, we risk loneliness, despair, and disconnection and all the negative health impacts of those.

Belonging is a powerful force. But what is it, really?

More than anything, belonging means listening deeply and building real relationships which go beyond surface interactions. This will look differently for every community, and I don't know exactly how it will look for yours. I encourage you to notice where your community makes you feel like you belong, and build belonging in those areas where it falls short. It will carry you in times of change and help you to support others when change comes for them.

Reflection Questions:

Do you have a group of people in your life to help you discern about big decisions?

Do you have community rituals for times of change?

How does your community support one another during times of change?

~ 17 ~

A QUICK-START GUIDE TO
FACING CHANGE

So... you are facing a big change right now. It may be expected or may have taken you absolutely by surprise. Whatever change you are facing, it will benefit you immensely if you become intentional about how you move through this period of change. Intentionality during times of change can not only make for a smoother transition to what lies beyond, but also lead to transformation. You can learn, grow, and change in positive ways.

This is fantastic news for you as you face this change! But it also means you have work to do.

Let's return to the rhythm that research suggests can help us find transformation in unexpected change. We begin with celebration and ritual, take time for reflection, and move into discernment for our new direction. If you like to figure out things on your own, try some or all of the techniques in those chapters to build your own rhythm.

Prefer a step-by-step list? I understand, I love those too, so here you go!

1. Name the thing that is changing in your life. Plan at least a dinner with friends and/or family to name it publicly, cele-

brate and bless what you are leaving behind, and light a candle of hope for all the new things that may come.

2. Plan some time daily to practice reflection. Put it on your calendar. Use the devotional journal included here, or get a blank journal and just dump all your thoughts there every day, until no more will come.

3. Add at least 5 minutes of silent stillness or mindfulness practice to that time. See what you hear.

4. Find a longer time for a retreat of sorts, a day off or a weekend. Spend the time in a park or a cabin without internet. Or sit out on your own front porch with no devices. Spend the day reading, reflecting and practicing mindfulness. Dig deep into any feelings of grief and shame, and make a list of ways you might process those emotions in healthy ways.

5. Begin to ask yourself questions about what may be next for you? What callings and hopes can you name? Journal these, and once they become solid enough, think about how to keep that future direction front and center. If nothing else, write it on a post-it and put it on your computer or front door so you see it every day.

6. Include your family and friends in these conversations about new directions. Listen to how the voice of calling may speak through them, and where you may need to practice healthy boundaries and relationship skills to best support one another

7. Find a way to mark and celebrate these hopes for the future. Gather your community and family together for a party, balloon release, or prayer circle to bless your new road.

Once you have incorporated this rhythm into times of change, opportunities abound! The change will be more successful, and learning is more likely to occur. Using the rhythm above will lay a foundation for you to survive and thrive in the face of whatever changes you are facing right now.

~ 18 ~

CULTIVATING CHANGE
READINESS

Even if you are not experiencing a big change right now, change is inevitable. This means that change readiness is crucial. When we are change-ready, we embrace changes when they come. We remember that God calls us to be willing to leave old roads behind. If we seek to become more change-ready, there are insights from the stories and seasons of Christian faith and from those who research and study change to help us along our way.

Going Deeper

Beyond the basics presented in the previous chapter for tackling unexpected changes as they arise, becoming intentional about learning and transformation on ordinary days can help you better handle change whenever it comes. Those ready to face change and transition with open minds and tools for learning will be most able to thrive.

I have good news: We can find transformation in any change, if we shape our lives in such a way as to be open to it. There are certain principles that research shows to be most important in becoming transformed by transitions. We can build these principles into our lives so that we are ready for change, whenever it comes. We may even get so skilled at change that we begin to seek it out as one of our spiritual practices.

Now that we know from the previous chapters what we need to be supported and transformed in their time of transition, how can we build these structures and practices into our lives, not just during times of active change, but in all seasons?

People, Get Ready

Advent is my favorite season of the church year. The themes of waiting and readiness do something in my heart. After 11 months of go-go-go, I find I need at least a month of wait to reset things. There is value in Advent waiting, beyond just its interruption of the frantic pace of modern life. However, Advent should not be the only time we consider the value of waiting and readiness as Christians. Readiness is a frequent theme in Jesus' teachings to his disciples. In the Gospel of Matthew, we find Jesus sharing parables about being ready.

> But about that day and hour no one knows, neither the angels of heaven, nor the Son, but only the Father. For as the days of Noah were, so will be the coming of the Son of Man. For as in those days before the flood they were eating and drinking, marrying and giving in marriage, until the day Noah entered the ark, and they knew nothing until the flood came and swept them all away, so too will be the coming of the Son of Man. Then two will be in the field; one will be taken and one will be left. Two women will be grinding meal together; one will be taken and one will be left. Keep awake therefore, for you do not know on what day your Lord is coming. But understand this: if the owner of the house had known in what part of the night the thief was coming, he would have stayed awake and would not have let his house be broken into. Therefore you also must be ready, for the Son of Man is coming at an unexpected hour. (Matthew 24:36-44)

Echoing the stories of the Hebrew Bible, when God's people were often surprised by the intervening hand of God, Jesus tells the disciples to be ready as they go about their normal daily activities. We cannot know when we will experience the inbreaking of God's presence, so we must remain ready and watchful as we go about our daily activities.

But what does that mean for us today? As Christians, we are called to set our hearts and minds in such a way as to be receptive to the inbreaking spirit of God. This can be one of the biggest challenges of our faith. Loving our neighbor is no picnic but being open to changing our preferences and routines is a whole other ball game. We all have opportunities to be transformed by the changes that come into our lives. Yet many of us, and many of the organizations we are a part of, remain stubbornly static, unchanged, and even raging against the change that comes to our doors. According to Musselwhite and Plouffe (2010), success in managing change and leveraging it for transformation requires us to "no longer view change as a discrete event to be managed, but as a constant opportunity to evolve."

Perhaps the most apt metaphor for readiness is that of hospitality. When you know someone may be coming over to visit, how do you prepare? Do you straighten up the house, make some tea or lemonade, prepare a few snacks? If you expect them overnight, do you put fresh sheets on the guest bed and give that room some extra attention? Maybe lay out a few towels for them or a robe? Getting ready for guests in our home is somewhat instinctual. We know what to do and just get to it when the time is right. And while most of us are not preparing for guests unless we know they are coming, some people are such masters of hospitality that their homes are always ready for whatever guest may happen by on any day. This mastery is the kind of readiness we can aim for in making ourselves ready for change.

Getting ready for change can be just as instinctual if we are practiced at it. The key is knowing what actions and elements make us ready. Just as fresh sheets and a pot of tea help welcome guests, there are certain characteristics and ways of being that help us welcome change whenever it comes our way.

Capacity, Commitment, Culture

Experts in organizational development typically measure change readiness by looking at whether an organization has the resources and skills available to navigate change, and enough cooperation and support from members to navigate change, and the capacity to devote enough energy to the change. Marge Combe (2014) suggests three indicators that serve to measure change readiness: Capacity, Commitment, and Culture. We can look at these three indicators in our own lives as well.

Change Culture is our openness to change in general and the ways our beliefs or values create positivity or resistance around change, from the smallest changes to the biggest. Culture also captures our ability to identify and name resistance and work past it, rather than seeing inner or external resistance as a reason to abandon the needed or inevitable change. Change culture also involves how the people and systems in our lives promote or block change. Are our friends and family supportive when we are trying to make a change? Are their attitudes toward change positive or negative? How about the systems in our lives -- do they allow us to change our roles and responsibilities when we need to make room for change? Are they rigid or flexible in terms of how we participate in or draw support from them?

Change Commitment is our willingness to adapt and change as needed in a changing world. While we don't have to be the biggest cheerleader of change, the quality we are looking for here is resolve: the resolve to stick with it and see things through in times of change, when challenging situations arise.

Change Capacity encompasses energy and time. When we are spread too thin or exhausted from doing too much, we will likely have greater difficulty with change.

These elements of readiness do not just happen spontaneously. We must create change-ready lives in order to find ongoing transformation in change. This is the way that we ensure that when change comes, we are ready. We need to cultivate the values of change readiness intentionally and openly. Combe also identifies several values that ground the culture of organizations who stay ready for change, which I have adapted and expanded upon for individuals.

Clear Mission and Values: Mission and values may sound like corporate words rather than something applicable to your individual life. And yet, our lives are constantly shaped by our sense of the ultimate mission of our time here on earth and by the values we hold most dear. What is your life's purpose? What values are most important to you? The answers to these questions are ever-changing, but if we don't ask them from time to time, we don't stand a chance of creating a life that has room for growth and change. This can also make it clearer why some changes are necessary. We are open to change when we see a need to align our lives with our values. We change more easily when we can see how the change might get us closer to our ultimate mission and purpose. We change when it is necessary to make our mission a reality.

Community: I can hear you now, we get it, community is important for change. I may be a broken record. But maybe you read the paragraph above and are wondering how to get a clear picture of your personal mission and values. Well, I have great news. Community can help with that, along with helping us navigate and grow from change. To figure out our core values, we need friends and family to listen with us to God's call for our lives. We also need their diverse perspectives and strategies when we are facing a big change. Finally, we need their moral and practical support when times get tough, and their presence at our rituals and celebrations in times of change. Finding your people, those that make up a community to accompany you in these ways, may make the difference between struggling with change and growing from it.

You may be saying that all sounds wonderful, but I am maxed out -- how do I get there from here? What would make my life more change-ready?

Time to Make a Change

Three key shifts in time and energy can make a huge impact on our change readiness.

End exhaustion: We are often spread too thin to consider any changes. Think of the way your job can feel when doing the work of two people due to vacancy or cutbacks. The mere idea of a new software system or form to complete to do your work feels overwhelming. We can be the same when facing life changes from a place of exhaustion. The only remedy for this is to cut back your life to the essentials, firstly those things that are necessary for health, safety and basic needs, with the addition of a few activities that align with your personal mission and values. It is a challenge to streamline but will pay dividends beyond imagining. Once you are less exhausted, you will be better able to consider and embrace change.

Create space for support: We are not alone on our journeys through change. Beyond exhaustion, constant activity can also make us too busy to connect with those who will be our companions through times of change. Find your people, and make time for them. One more task checked off the list is less important than building a fabric of support for any change you are facing now or will face in the future.

Make room for reflection: Too often, our busy lives are filled with activities that, if initially well-intentioned, can become mechanical and rote. Make space in your daily activities for pauses, meditation, prayer. Our best energy and ideas often come from a place of centeredness within us, one that is difficult to find if we are constantly in motion. Focus on the role of spirit in your life. Take time for reflecting, between activities and at the end of the day, on where God can be seen in your life. Use your community for reflection with others. These practices will give you practice in how to listen to

Spirit. This cycle of action and reflection will give you ears to hear how God might be present in change, and open your eyes to see where change might be transforming you and your spiritual journey. Open eyes and listening ears will keep you ready for a visit from change, whether you know it is coming or not.

The work of cultivating change readiness is worthwhile, even as a million other things fill our to-do lists. If you pause some of that frenetic activity to make your life ready for whatever changes may come, you will be that much less likely to be derailed on the day they arrive. This effort will pay off in so many ways. Knowing and doing all this does not make it easy when life events or a call from God sets us off down a completely different road. However, it can help us travel that hard road.

Reflection Questions:

Where are you thriving in the areas described above? Which areas need attention?

How can you build change readiness in your life right now? What practical steps can you take this week? This month? This year?

~ 19 ~

CONCLUSION

Are you ready?

Are you ready to celebrate and try new rituals?

Are you ready to accept your situation as it is?

Are you ready to take time for mindfulness, sabbath and reflection?

Are you ready to face the challenges of grief, shame, and varying levels of support from community and family?

Are you ready to listen, to discern, to hear the voice of what is next for you?

Are you ready to become a person who not only navigates change successfully but also one who can grow from it personally and spiritually?

If so, if you are willing to take on this challenge, you and our world as a whole will be better for it.

The tools provided in this book are designed to help you begin to use these practices as a part of your life. However, I would encourage you to not stop there. Stay creative. Play with mindfulness and ritual. Preach radical acceptance that fuels action. Share your gifts and strengthen your community. That way, if tomorrow is the day that you face unexpected change, you will be ready to embrace the change and hear where God speaks in transition time. In short, you will be ready for whatever the future may hold.

Here is where I leave you, for now. The road is ready. Your bags are packed with everything you need for the journey. I pray that you will find along the way all the insights, growth, and spiritual presence you need to live fully into all that lies ahead. With your new knowledge, open eyes and listening ears, I just know that you can find transformation in any change headed your way.

~ 20 ~

FINDING TRANSFORMATION IN UNEXPECTED CHANGE: A 31-DAY JOURNAL

Diving deeper into our own feelings and experiences of change can help equip us to better navigate future changes. Take a few minutes every day to write about the journal prompt in the space provided or in your own journal/notebook. Share insights you find in this process with friends and family, when you can.

Day 1: How do you feel when things in your life change? Are you thrown for a loop? Or do you love that feeling of navigating new territory?

DAY 2

Describe a recent change you faced. How did it feel at the time?

DAY 3

When was the last time you threw a party to celebrate something new? What was the occasion?

DAY 4

Who in your life can help you discern about big decisions? How do you engage their help when facing change?

DAY 5

Who in your life would you say you know deeply? Who knows you deeply?

DAY 6

How well do you know your neighbors? What could help with that?

DAY 7

What is your favorite Bible verse or story about change? Why?

DAY 8

Do you practice Sabbath? How?

DAY 9

What practices of rest and restoration can you draw on during times of change?

DAY 10

When was the last time you paused all your activities for a day or longer? What was that like?

Do you have any rituals you use in times of change? If so, describe them and why they are meaningful to you? If not, what could help you find some?

DAY 12

How does your circle of friends and family provide support to one another during times of change?

DAY 13

What might shift for you if you cultivated radical acceptance?

DAY 14

What changes do you remember facing in your childhood?

DAY 15

Are there children in your life? What changes are they facing right now? (Or, what do you imagine are the most common changes children deal with?)

DAY 16

What would have been helpful in learning about change in your younger years? How might you offer that to today's young people?

DAY 17

When is the last time you tried something new for fun or pleasure? What does it feel like to try new things?

DAY 18

What change is most present in your life right now? How is that change challenging? How is it exciting?

DAY 19

Describe a time that you found good news or encountered God in an unexpected change.

DAY 20

What change would be a gift to you right now?

Do you talk to your friends and family about times when you encounter God in change? If so, what is that like for you? If not, what could help you be more open about those experiences?

DAY 22

What might you need to let go of to make room for change?

What might you need to let go of to make room for change?

DAY 24

What support do you need to say goodbye to something that no longer serves you?

DAY 25

How might you celebrate and honor those things you must let go for
the new to come into being?

DAY 26

What are you most fearful about in terms of change in your life right now?

DAY 27

What are your greatest hopes for your life in the next year? In the next 5 years?

DAY 28

What in your life or local community are you most passionate about right now? How has that changed over time?

DAY 29

What in your past has prepared you for times of change? When have you navigated change successfully? What helped you do that?

DAY 30

What gifts do you have that can help you navigate change? What do you need to access and use those gifts?

DAY 31

What people are in your life that can support you in times of change?
What do you need to bring them into the journey with you?

Bibliography

While it would be impossible to capture each and every text or resource that influenced the development of my ideas about change, the following list includes those cited in this book as well as other resources that were particularly helpful to me along the way. I encourage you to dive into some of this material if you would like to go deeper into the research and theories around finding transformation in change.

All scripture quotations are from the New Revised Standard Version Bible, copyright © 1989 National Council of the Churches of Christ in the United States of America. Used by permission. All rights reserved worldwide.

Alo House Recovery Centers. Infographic - How a sense of community belonging impacts the brain. https://alorecovery.com/community-belonging-infographic/

Alonderienė, R. & Pundzienė, A. (2008). The significance of formal, informal and non-formal learning for the acquisition of the change management competence. *Vocational Education: Research & Reality, 15* (2008), 173-180.

Baldwin, L. V., & Anderson, V. (2019). *Revives my soul again.* Project Muse.

Bailey, L. (2015). Belonging revolution giving life to new community narrative. https://www.abundantcommunity.com/the-belonging-revolution-giving-life-to-a-new-community-narrative/. April 27, 2015.

Baskette. M. P. (2015). *Standing naked before God: The art of public confession.* Cleveland: Pilgrim Press.

Block, P. (2008). *Community: The structure of belonging.* San Francisco: Berrett—Koehler Publishers.

Brach, T. (2003). *Radical acceptance: Embracing your life with the heart of a Buddha.* New York: Bantam.

Bridges, W. (1991). *Managing transitions: Making the most of change.* Reading, Mass: Addison-Wesley.

brown, a. m. (2017). *Emergent strategy: Shaping change, changing worlds.* Chico, CA: AK Press.

Brown, B. (2017). *Braving the wilderness: The quest for true belonging and the courage to stand alone.* New York: Random House.

Butler Bass, D. (2012). *Christianity after religion: The end of church and the birth of a new spiritual awakening.* Kindle Edition, New York: HarperCollins.

Church, F. (2008). *Love and death: My journey through the valley of the shadow.* Boston: Beacon Press.

Combe, M. (2014). Change readiness: Focusing change management where it counts," *Project Management Institute,* July 2014, https://www.pmi.org/learning/library/change-readiness-11126.

Community Health and Wellbeing: Shift the Conversation, an initiative of the Association of Ontario Health Centers (2015). The belonging guide: Exploring the importance of belonging to good health. http://communityhealthandwellbeing.org/resources/belonging_guide

Coyle, D. (2018). *The culture code: The secrets of highly successful groups.* New York: Bantam Books.

Duncan, L. E. (1999), Motivation for collective action: Group consciousness as mediator of personality, life experiences, and women's rights activism. *Political Psychology, 20*: 611-635. doi:10.1111/0162-895X.00159

Fleischer, B. J. (2006). "The ministering community as context for religious education: A case study of St. Gabriel's catholic parish," *Religious Education, 101*(1), 104-122.

Gilster, M. E. (2012), Comparing neighborhood-focused activism and volunteerism: Psychological well-being and social connectedness. *Journal of Community Psychology, 40*: 769-784. doi:10.1002/jcop.20528

Hammond, C. (1994). *Stories to hold an audience.* Newtown, NSW: Millennium Books.

Hofmann, S. G. & Gómez, A. F. (2017). Mindfulness-based interventions for anxiety and depression. *The Psychiatric Clinics of North America, 40*(4), 739-749.

Itzhaky, H., Zanbar, L., Levy, D. & Schwartz, C. (2015). The contribution of personal and community resources to well-being and sense of belonging to the community among community activists. *The British Journal of Social Work,* *45*(6), 1678–1698, https://doi.org/10.1093/bjsw/bct176

Jordan, C. (1970 Original; 2004 Edition currently available). The Cotton Patch Version of Matthew and John. Macon, GA: Smyth & Helwys. https://www.helwys.com/sh-books/the-cotton-patch-gospel-4/

Kissell, K., Moser, K.S., & Dubowski, J. (2017). *Enhancing ministry & improving clergy well-being: Exploring the impact of Bowen's Systems Coaching on the work-related psychological health of clergy.* Paper presented at British Psychological Society: Division of Counselling Psychology Annual Conference, Stratford Upon Avon, UK, 07 July 2017 - 08 July 2017. London South Bank University.

Landgraf, D., Long, J., Der-Avakian, A., et al. (2015). Dissociation of learned helplessness and fear conditioning in mice: a mouse model of depression. *PloS One, 10*(4) e0125892

Lederach, J. P. (2005). *The moral imagination: The art and soul of building peace,* Oxford: Oxford University Press.

Levy, D. , Itzhaky, H. , Zanbar, L. & Schwartz, C. (2012). Sense Of cohesion among community activists engaging in volunteer activity. *Journal of Community Psychology, 40*: 735-746. doi:10.1002/jcop.21487

Lewis, S. H. & Kraut, R. E. (1972). Correlates of student political activism and ideology. *Journal of Social Issues,* 28: 131-149. doi:10.1111/ j.1540-4560.1972.tb00051.x

Major, J. S., Queen, S., Meyer, A., & Roth, H. D., Trans. (2010). *The Huainanzi: A guide to the theory and practice of government in early Han China* (Translations from the Asian Classics). Columbia University Press.

McClerking, H. K & McDaniel, E. L. (2005). Belonging and doing: Political churches and black political participation. *Political Psychology,* 26: 721-734. doi:10.1111/j.1467-9221.2005.00441.x

McLaren, B. (2015). *We make the road by walking: A year-long quest for spiritual formation, reorientation, and activation.* London: Hodder.

Mead, L. B. (2005). *A change of pastors: ...And how it affects change in the congregation.* Bethesda, MD: Alban Institute.

Mezirow, J. (2000). Learning to think like an adult. In Mezirow, J. & Associates (Eds), *Learning as transformation: Critical perspectives on a theory in progress* (pp. 3-33). San Francisco, CA: Jossey-Bass.

Musselwhite, C. & Plouffe, T. (2011). Communicating change as business as usual. *Harvard Business Review Blog Network*, July 19, 2011, http://blogs.hbr.org/cs/2011/07/communicating_change_as_ busine.html

Mosher, L. (2005). *Faith in the neighborhood: Belonging.* New York: Church Publishing.

Neal, D. T., Wood, W., Wu, M. et al. (2011). The pull of the past: When do habits persist despite conflict with motives?" *Personality and Social Psychology Bulletin, 37*(11), 1428-1437.

Newbert, A. & Waldman, R. (2010*). How God changes your brain: Breakthrough findings from a leading neuroscientist.* New York: Ballantine Books.

Norton, M. I. & Gino, F. (2014). Rituals alleviate grieving for loved ones, lovers, and lotteries. *Journal of Experimental Psychology: General, 143*(1), 266 –272.

Omoto, A. M., Snyder, M. & Hackett, J. D. (2010), Personality and motivational antecedents of activism and civic engagement. *Journal of Personality,* 78: 1703-1734. doi:10.1111/j.1467-6494.2010.00667.x

Ornish, D., Scherwitz, L. W., Billings, J. H. et al (1998). Intensive lifestyle changes for reversal of coronary heart disease. *JAMA, 280*(23), 2001–2007.

Percival, A. (2016). Benefits of belonging. HuffPost. October 17, 2016. https://www.huffingtonpost.com/entry/benefits-of-belonging_us_580519e1e4b06f314afeb8d0

Pogosyan, M. (2017). On belonging. *Psychology Today.* April 11, 2017. https://www.psychologytoday.com/us/blog/between-cultures/201704/belonging

Rearick, S. (2017). Time banks: A tool for restorative justice and community strength, *HuffPost*, December 7, 2017, www.huffpost.com/entry/time-banks-a-tool-for-res_b_6754292.

Reddy, K. (2011). Benefits of belonging: Dynamic group identity as a protective resource against psychological threat. Dissertation, Columbia University. https://core.ac.uk/download/pdf/161440654.pdf

Rock, D. (2008). SCARF: a brain-based model for collaborating with and influencing others. *NeuroLeadership Journal,* 1.

Rohr, R. (2016). Your life is not about you (Adapted from Richard Rohr, *Adam's Return: The Five Promises of Male Initiation*, The Crossroad Publishing Company: 2004, 62-64, 66). Center for Action and Contemplation. May 25, 2016. Accessed at https://cac.org/your-life-is-not-about-you-2016-05-25/

Ross, H. J. & Tartaglione, J. (2018). *Our search for belonging: How our need to connect is tearing us apart.* Oakland, CA: Berrett-Koehler Publishers, Inc.

Rumi, S. (2004). *Rumi: Selected Poem* (Coleman Barks with J. Moynce, A. J. Arberry, R. Nicholson, Trans.). New York: Penguin Books.

Scarlett, H. (2016). *Neuroscience for organizational change: An evidence-based practical guide to managing change.* New York: Kogen Page Limited.

Seibert, S. E., Kraimer, M. L., Holtom, B. C. et al. (2013). Even the best laid plans sometimes go askew: Career self-management processes, career shocks, and the decision to pursue graduate education. *Journal of Applied Psychology, 98* (1), 169-182.

Smillie, R.L. (2011). *Practicing reverence: An ethic for sustainable earth communities.* Kelowna, BC: Copperhouse.

Taylor, V. A., Grant, J., Daneault, V. et al. (2011). Impact of mindfulness on the neural responses to emotional pictures in experienced and beginner meditators. *NeuroImage, 57,* 1524-1533.

Ter Kuile, C. & Thurston, A. (2015). *How We Gather.* Cambridge, MA: Harvard Divinity School.

Ter Kuile, C., Phillips, S. & Thurston, A. (2015). *Care of Souls.* Cambridge, MA: Harvard Divinity School.

Thomas, L., Herbert, J. & Teras, M. (2014). A sense of belonging to enhance participation, success and retention in online programs. *The International Journal of the First Year in Higher Education, 5*(2), 69-80. doi: 10.5204/intjfyhe.v5i2.233

Vaccaro, A. & Mena, J. A. (2011). It's not burnout, *it's more:* Queer college activists of color and mental health. *Journal of Gay & Lesbian Mental Health, 15*(4), 339-367, DOI: 10.1080/19359705.2011.600656

Vogl, C. (2016). *The art of community: Seven principles for belonging.* Oakland, CA: Berrett-Koehler Publishers.

Watkins, K. E. & Marsick, V. J. (2010). Group and organizational learning. In *Handbook of Adult and Continuing Education,* Kasworm, Carol E., et al (Eds.). Thousand Oaks, CA: SAGE, 59-70.

Ziegler, M. (1999). "Awakening": Developing learning capacity in a small family business. *Advances in Developing Human Resources, 1,* 52 - 65.

Weller, F. (2015). *The Wild Edge of Sorrow: Rituals of Renewal and the Sacred Work of Grief* (Berkeley, CA: North Atlantic Books.

Westen, D., Blagov, P. S., Harenski, K. et al. (2006). Neural bases of motivated reasoning: An fMRI study of emotional constraints on partisan political judgment in the 2004 U.S. presidential election. *Journal of Cognitive Neuroscience, 18*(11), 1947-1957

Zhao, L., Lu, Y., Wang, B. et al. (2012). Cultivating the sense of belonging and motivating user participation in virtual communities: A social capital perspective, *International Journal of Information Management, 32*(6), 574-588, ISSN 0268-4012, https://doi.org/10.1016/j.ijinfomgt.2012.02.006.

Anna Mitchell Hall is an ordained Baptist minister who has coordinated programs and conducted research in churches, nonprofits, and universities. In her work as Director of Research and Development for ConvergenceUS.org, she draws on the latest research from across the fields of religious practice, organizational development, and adult learning to inform product development and implementation that supports the needs of pastors and churches. She holds a Master of Divinity from Candler School of Theology, Emory University, a Master of Public Administration from Valdosta State University, and a Ph.D. from the University of Georgia, where her research focused on congregations experiencing a change in pastors. Find Anna at:

https://www.facebook.com/changereadychristians
https://twitter.com/annamhall
https://www.linkedin.com/in/annamitchellhall

A Note from Anna

What did you think of Life After?

I am so grateful that among all the books in the world, you took the time to read mine. I hope it was helpful to you as you navigate change in your life and the lives of your loved ones. If so, I would love it if you could share it with those in your life by posting about it on social media. I also invite you to tag me or my social media pages so I can like and share your post.

If you did find the book valuable, I would also love to hear from you about that experience. Your feedback is very important to me and will also help me spread the word about my books. You can post a review on Amazon or Goodreads at the following links:
https://www.amazon.com/dp/B09LQRZXQH
https://www.goodreads.com/book/show/59631761-life-after

Please reach out if you are interested in help navigating change. I am available for coaching, church consulting, or speaking engagements. Thank you again for reading.

Do you have a book that you would like to get out into the world? Cane Mill Press, a small hybrid publisher, is seeking new authors of spiritual nonfiction, memoir, and cozy mysteries. Contact editor@canemillpress.com for more information.

curated fiction and nonfiction
rooted in south Georgia, branching beyond

CPSIA information can be obtained
at www.ICGtesting.com
Printed in the USA
BVHW072038141221
624005BV00022B/927

9 781737 560425